THINKING SMARTER

THINKING
SMARTER

Seven Steps to Your
Fulfilling Retirement . . . and Life

SHLOMO BENARTZI with ROGER LEWIN

PORTFOLIO / PENGUIN

The authors believe the principles and strategies suggested by this book will contribute to improving outcomes for retirees by helping them set clear goals and make better decisions. However, this material does not constitute legal or tax advice and does not address the issues associated with implementing any recommendations. There are many legal and tax implications to consider and qualified advisers should be consulted before any particular strategy is implemented. The book contains the current opinions of the authors, which are subject to change without notice and do not necessarily reflect the views of Allianz Global Investors and its affiliates.

References to financial instruments are for illustrative purposes only and are not intended to be, and should not be interpreted as, recommendations to purchase or sell such securities. Investing in any security involves risk, including loss of principal. No strategy assures success or protects against loss, nor is past performance a guarantee of future results.

References to specific websites are for informational purposes only and do not represent an endorsement of the source company, its products or services.

The Center for Behavioral Finance is sponsored by Allianz Global Investors U.S. LLC and Allianz Global Investors Distributors LLC.

PORTFOLIO / PENGUIN

Published by the Penguin Publishing Group
Penguin Random House LLC
375 Hudson Street
New York, New York 10014

USA | Canada | UK | Ireland | Australia
New Zealand | India | South Africa | China
penguin.com
A Penguin Random House Company

First published by Portfolio / Penguin, an imprint of Penguin Publishing Group, a division of Penguin Random House LLC, 2015

ISBN 978-1-59184-805-9

Printed in the United States of America
10 9 8 7 6 5 4 3 2 1

Set in Janson Text LT Std
Designed by Neuwirth & Associates, Inc.

ACKNOWLEDGMENTS

Writing books is typically something of a collective effort, with the author benefiting from helpful input and suggestions from many people. This one is no exception.

First, I should like to acknowledge the help of a wonderful group of academic advisers, which includes Richard Thaler, Daniel Goldstein, Peter Ayton, and, especially, John Payne, who can always be relied upon to see right to the nub of any tangled issue.

Dozens of financial advisers, and a smaller number of individuals on the point of retirement, provided invaluable insights based on their experience of the challenge of planning for retirement.

This book was developed by the Allianz Global Investors Center for Behavioral Finance and its skillful and enthusiastic team as part of a broader project focused on helping people make the most of their retirement years. Thank you Steve Shu, Kim Andranovich, Caitlin Ledwith, Namika Sagara, and, most of all, Cathy Smith, director of the Center. And thanks, too, to Brian Gaffney for his ongoing vital encouragement and support.

Last, but not least, it is my joy to thank my wife, Lesli, and Maya, our now-not-so-little girl, for their love and supportive presence through this intense book-writing process.

CONTENTS

THINKING SMARTER

Introduction

I am a behavioral economist with a bad back. (Don't worry: This book is not about chronic back problems.) The problem with having a bad back is obvious: pain. The solution, however, is far less obvious. Fixing a bad back requires experimentation and the patience to figure out what helps relieve the pain and what doesn't. Your doctors have to balance multiple competing goals: how to seek a reduction in pain with the fewest possible side effects at the lowest possible cost, not to mention the fact that medical treatments require personalization, because what works for me might not work for you and vice versa. Finally, a successful solution will most likely involve multiple treatments. Maybe you'll need surgery followed by physical therapy, or medication and a new pair of shoes. It is often not the individual treatments that make the difference but rather the *portfolio* of treatments, including how to orchestrate their timing.

I'm telling you about my back because dealing with behavioral challenges is very much like treating back pain. Similar to back pain, the problems are often obvious. For example, we spend and eat too much but save and exercise too little. However, solutions to these problems are far less obvious. The fixes for behavioral problems also require personalization, as different people will require different treatments. For instance, what helps my wife eat less (early dinners) differs from what helps me eat less (sharing my croissant with the barista, so I only eat half). Effective solutions for behavioral challenges, be they financial or health choices, often require more than one trick, just as with treatments for back pain. Eating early does help my wife, but we might need to skip desserts as well if we really want to accomplish our goals. (Ouch.)

This book is about using the behavioral economics tool set—a tool set that comprises many distinct behavioral insights—to help people think and choose wisely. It is not the individual insights that are at the core of this book, but rather our attempt to use a large *portfolio* of tools to help you make good decisions, just as a good doctor would treat a bad back. By helping a lot of people think and choose wisely, I hope we can not only improve their lives but also solve some big societal problems.

Let me begin with a proof of concept that illustrates how one behavioral economics tool set has already helped millions of people double their retirement saving rates. Back in 1996, Richard Thaler and I designed a program to help employees save more for retirement. We were concerned that in the new world of 401(k) plans (old-fashioned pension plans were on their way out rapidly), employees were not saving enough on their own. This is still a significant problem, as 68 percent of employees say they should save more, and of those who say they plan to save more in the near future, most fail to do anything about it (Choi et al., 2002).

Very much like a doctor, we began by trying to understand the source of the problem. In our case, instead of looking at MRIs of the spine, we examined the behavioral challenges that prevent people from following up on their good intentions to save more. The key takeaway we learned was that there isn't just one behavioral challenge to be addressed in making choices, but many. (A few examples of these behavioral challenges include present bias, loss aversion, inertia, and procrastination.)

The behavioral solution we crafted, called Save More Tomorrow™, had an overarching idea to make the act of saving as easy as possible (Thaler and Benartzi, 2004). We accomplished this by changing the choice environment, or "choice architecture," as Richard Thaler and Cass Sunstein call it in their influential book *Nudge* (Thaler and Sunstein, 2009). Accordingly, our program placed employees on an autopilot path that boosted their saving rates every time they got a pay raise—the pain of saving more was numbed by timing it with raises in pay. By 2011, we were fortunate enough to have doubled the saving rates of more than four million employees in the US (Benartzi and Thaler, 2013).

While the program seems intuitive and straightforward, it is very important to note that it includes *multiple* features and behavioral insights, from addressing inertia and procrastination by setting an autopilot feature, to handling the pain of saving more by waiting for a pay raise. The lesson? By using multiple insights from our behavioral economics tool set we can design behavioral interventions that make a big difference.

In this book, I'd like to address a related problem: how to identify both your goals and what is important to you in retirement in order to begin the process of achieving those goals. This is a major societal challenge because, over the next two decades, about seventy million baby boomers are set to retire and these retirees will need to be able to answer these questions (Pew Research Center, 2010). That amounts to 10,000 new retirees a day. Globally, I am guesstimating that more than one billion people will retire over the next couple of decades. But it is not only the volume of new retirees that makes retirement planning an important issue—it is also the complexity of the problem.

For one thing, retirement involves a lot of risks. Some risks are obvious, such as losing money in the stock market. Other risks are less obvious but just as important. For example, what if you win the "longevity lottery" and live to one hundred? One study in the UK estimates that one-third of recent newborns there will live to one hundred. The question is, how will people pay for such a long retirement? (UK Office for National Statistics, 2013). Another, but less obvious risk of retirement, is cognitive impairment, as about 50 percent of people in their eighties have some kind of cognitive impairment and are not in a good position to make sound financial decisions (Agarwal et al., 2009). And, of course, we also have to consider health risks, since out-of-pocket medical expenses can easily add up to hundreds of thousands of dollars (Webb and Zhivan, 2010).

The complexity of retirement gets magnified by individual differences. The behavioral prescription for college grads who need to save for retirement is pretty simple: Get a job and stick to the Save More Tomorrow™ program. As people age, however, individual differences proliferate, and this "one shoe fits all" approach is no longer appropriate. For example, think of health. Most college grads are young and healthy with minor individual differences in health. By the time they reach retirement, however, those individual differences will often prove huge. My dad, who will soon turn seventy-eight, is on the treadmill every day for thirty minutes and is in good shape. My father-in-law, who is more than ten years younger, has already experienced multiple heart attacks and suffers from diabetes. The differences across people are, of course, not just about their circumstances but also about who they are and what they love doing. My father-in-law, for example, loves fishing, whereas my dad hates fishing (I can't even get him to eat fish).

To highlight just how different people are as they navigate the retirement journey, I'll use two case studies throughout this book. One is about "Francesca," a successful executive about to turn fifty. The other is about "Phillip,"* a professor who is still working as he nears seventy but debating whether there is a new career or some other dramatic change waiting for him around the corner.

So, what can be done to help Francesca, Phillip and the seventy million baby boomers make the most of their retirement? In order to accommodate these dramatic individual differences, we must tailor the solution to the circumstances and preferences of each person. One approach is to help people by using a process called "thinking architecture." It is a structured process that allows us to break down a complex problem, such as what to do in retirement, into a series of manageable thinking steps, so as to improve outcomes. What makes these steps different from traditional checklists is that each of them is designed to deal with a particular behavioral challenge or mental blind spot. My advice, in other words, is designed to fortify the weakest parts of the mind.

I know it might feel awkward to seek help "thinking." After all, we should already know how to think by the time we're past middle age. But don't feel bad—although we have been blessed with a very powerful thinking machine, there's good evidence that we don't like to use it, at least to

---

* Francesca and Phillip are pseudonyms but their stories are real.

introspect on our life situation. For instance, in one recent experiment, researchers at Harvard University and the University of Virginia offered volunteers across a wide age range the opportunity to sit quietly by themselves for six to fifteen minutes, the only demand being that they be quiet and think (Wilson et al., 2014). This proved to be too much for many people. Two-thirds of the men chose to give themselves at least one electric shock during the test period in order to avoid thinking. (One man, an outlier, delivered 190 such shocks in a fifteen-minute period!) Women were much less averse to thinking and only a quarter of them sought other distractions. The bottom line, however, is that we humans tend to be cognitively lazy and often try to avoid thinking altogether.

You can see, then, that thinking smartly—or even at all—is a challenge. As we move through the following chapters, you will learn that even when people are highly motivated to think about what is important to them, they still tend to think too fast or not deeply and broadly enough. For instance, research shows that even when people think long and hard about goals that are relevant to a weighty decision, they typically miss about half of what, with help, they eventually come to identify as being really important to them (Bond, Carlson, and Keeney, 2008).

You might be familiar with some of the behavioral challenges covered in this book, perhaps from reading great books like Thaler and Sunstein's *Nudge*, Daniel Kahneman's *Thinking, Fast and Slow* (Kahneman, 2011), and Chip and Dan Heath's *Decisive* (Heath and Heath, 2013). This short book is in the same genre but goes further in that it attempts to put multiple behavioral solutions together into a system that helps us think better about our goals, whichever complex decisions we face.

This book will help you think more effectively about what you want in your retirement. Of course, there are a lot of aspects to retirement to think about. Research suggests that when tackling any major decision you should start with understanding your goals. If you think of retirement as a journey, then a logical starting point is to figure out who you are, what you care about, and where you're trying to go. I will help you identify your retirement goals by offering a seven-step thinking process called the Goal Planning System (or GPS), which addresses a variety of thinking challenges.

The book is composed of seven chapters with each chapter covering one step of the seven-step thinking process. More specifically, each chapter, or step, will highlight a common behavioral challenge and then describe the thinking tool necessary to overcome the challenge.

After you have been through the seven steps of the GPS exercise (Steps 1–7), you will read how Francesca and Phillip translated their newly prioritized goals into next-step action items, which I frame as general lessons for all retirees to consider. There is also a short summary chapter for quick reference; a short afterword that looks briefly at the application of behavioral science and behavioral economics beyond setting goals; and an appendix that will help you begin a conversation about your goals for retirement, should you decide to recruit the help of a financial adviser in taking concrete steps toward achieving your goals.

While this book focuses on retirement, you will also meet my very good friend David and learn how he used the GPS process to think smarter about a very different challenge: deciding where he wants to settle down. With this book as your guide, you can learn to think smarter when making important life decisions.

So, for Francesca, for Phillip, for David, for you—if you want to think smarter about your important life journeys, then this book is for you.

GOAL PLANNING SYSTEM

If your primary interest is in planning for retirement and you want to go through the Goal Planning System process, or if you simply wish to see GPS in action with a real-world problem, the GPS tool is available as a free Apple iPad application for use by individuals and financial professionals. For more information on the application, please visit:

http://www.retirementgoalplanningsystem.com.

There you will find some background information on the system itself, an electronic version of the GPS tool that takes you through the seven steps for retirement, and other support materials (such as printable versions of some of the tools if you do not have access to a supported device for the electronic version of the GPS tool).

REFERENCES

Agarwal, Sumit, John C. Driscoll, Xavier Gabaix, and David Laibson. 2009 (Fall). "The Age of Reason: Financial Decisions over the Life-Cycle with Implications for

Regulation," Brookings Papers on Economic Activity. 51–117.

Benartzi, Shlomo, and Richard H. Thaler. 2013. "Behavioral Economics and the Retirement Savings Crisis." *Science* 339: 1152–1153.

Bond, Samuel D., Kurt A. Carlson, and Ralph L. Keeney. 2008. "Generating Objectives: Can Decision Makers Articulate What They Want?" *Management Science* 54, no 1: 56–70.

Choi, James J., David Laibson, Brigitte C. Madrian, and Andrew Metrick. 2002. "Defined Contribution Pensions: Plan Rules, Participant Decisions, Choices, and the Path of Least Resistance." *Tax Policy and the Economy* vol. 16, James Poterba, ed., Cambridge, MA: MIT Press: 67–113.

Heath, Chip, and Dan Heath. 2013. *Decisive: How to Make Better Decisions in Life and Work*. New York: Crown Business Books.

Kahneman, Daniel. 2011. *Thinking, Fast and Slow*. New York: Farrar, Straus and Giroux.

Pew Research Center. 2010. "Baby Boomers Retire." Daily Number, December 29.

Thaler, Richard H., and Shlomo Benartzi. 2004. "Save More Tomorrow™: Using Behavioral Economics to Increase Employee Saving." *Journal of Political Economy* 112, no. 1, part 2: §164–187.

Thaler, Richard H., and Cass R. Sunstein. 2009. *Nudge: Improving Decisions About Health, Wealth, and Happiness*. New York: Penguin.

UK Office for National Statistics. 2013. "One Third of Babies Born in 2013 Are Expected to Live to 100," http://www .ons.gov.uk/ons/rel/lifetables/historic-and-projected-data -from-the-period-and-cohort-life-tables/2012-based/sty -babies-living-to-100.html.

Webb, Anthony, and Natalia A. Zhivan. 2010. "What Is the Distribution of Lifetime Health Care Costs from Age 65?" Issue in Brief 10–4, Center for Retirement Research at Boston College.

Wilson, Timothy D., David A. Reinhard, Erin C. Westgate, Daniel T. Gilbert, Nicole Ellerbeck, Cheryl Hahn, Casey L. Brown, and Adi Shaked. 2014. "Just Think: The Challenges of the Disengaged Mind." *Science* 345: 75–77.

STEP 1

Identify Your Goals

Y ou and your partner have just finished a delicious meal at one of your favorite restaurants and you are deep into a conversation on the topic that greatly interests both of you: local politics. The waiter appears at your table and unobtrusively clears the remnants of your entrée, pours the remaining wine into your glasses, and goes to the waiters' station. After a few minutes he returns to your table, engages your attention, and asks, "Can I interest you in dessert this evening?" You both indicate that you might well be interested. The waiter hands you the menu: Chocolate Mousse, a Selection of Sorbets, Apple Pie, Crème Brûlée. Tempting, as usual.

What to choose? You examine the offerings, trying to decide which to select and share. Should it be the chocolate mousse? You know it is always excellent. "No, we had that the last time we were here," you say. How about the apple pie? "Maybe it'd be a little too filling," says your partner. Your partner then says, "Look, crème brûlée, that's new on the menu here. Why don't we try that?"

What do you do?

Behavioral Challenge:
Alternative Thinking

When any of us faces a choice, there is a strong tendency to get caught in a well-recognized thinking trap. Namely, we laser in on the alternatives that come easily to mind, such as the ones directly in front of us, and immediately begin to weigh their pros and cons. In so doing, we ignore other aspects of the decision that may be important to us but aren't immediately obvious.

This thinking trap is what decision scientist Ralph Keeney has labeled Alternative-Focused Thinking (Keeney, 1992a). We find alternative thinking very attractive, irresistible even, for two reasons: First, it happens naturally; second, it is what we learn as we go through life. Let me explain.

You will recall that I said in the introduction that one of the behavioral challenges we face in making decisions is sometimes thinking too fast. Fast thinking is concrete and "now oriented," so that when faced with choices it leads us to jump rapidly to evaluating alternatives directly in front of us or that come readily to mind.

The second reason we find alternative thinking so compelling flows from what we learn as we go through life.

Making good decisions is a formidable challenge. The process is more complex than most skills we tackle in life because there are many psychological traps that can derail our thinking. And, despite its importance in many realms of our lives, very few people receive any formal instruction in how to make good decisions. It's like that other vital activity in life that many of us face with absolutely no training: being a parent. If you are a parent, you know exactly what I mean. You are expected to learn as you go along and hope you don't make too many dreadful mistakes on the way.

In the realm of decision making, what we learn as we go along is that making decisions is about choosing between alternatives (Keeney, 2004). Do I want to go to a movie tonight or do I want to eat out at a restaurant instead? Shall we take our vacation in the mountains or go to the beach? Which of two terrific job offers should I accept? The one in New York City with the attractive salary but not-so-great climate? Or the one in Los Angeles, which has a lower salary but where the weather is much better? Should I save for my retirement or buy that sports car and enjoy my money while I can? And so on.

Alternative thinking is therefore a very familiar process to each of us.

As a result, when you and your partner are poring over that dessert menu, your focus is "chocolate mousse, a selection of sorbets, apple pie, crème brûlée, hmm, what'll it be?" You tend *not* to think, for instance, "How about skipping dessert completely, because we want to enjoy the health benefits of consuming fewer calories than we would otherwise. Or perhaps we should go to that great coffee shop across the street and finish our conversation there." You don't consider these other possibilities because you are focused on what is in front of you.

You don't realize that in focusing on the options that are immediately in front of you, you may unwittingly be excluding other relevant possibilities.

Behavioral Solution:
Employ Value Thinking

"Alternative-Focused Thinking is a limited way to think through decisions," says Keeney. "It is reactive, not proactive. . . . This standard model of thinking is backward, because it puts the cart of identifying alternatives before the horse of articulating values" (Keeney, 1992b). As a consequence, when you go down the path of alternative thinking in making decisions, you are likely to end up with an incomplete set of alternatives, or goals, to consider. More important, you have no way of knowing whether the options you are weighing reflect what you value most. As Keeney put it: "To enhance the likelihood that you will get what you want, it is important—perhaps essential—to know what you want" (Keeney, 1992c).

Keeney's behavioral solution to the shortcomings of alternative thinking is what he calls, not too surprisingly, Value-Focused Thinking. When making a decision, you have to have a series of alternatives to choose from but the principle of value thinking is that alternatives are the means by which you achieve what you value. And the process of value thinking is that you focus first on values, that is, on what is important to you, and then on the alternatives that will help you achieve those goals. In other words, values are what you care about, they define who you are and what you aspire to be. In value thinking, values are what drive the decision-making process.

The cynic might say, "Oh, yes, values. Sounds nice. Warm and fuzzy even. But is it an *effective* means of making important decisions?" The answer is, Yes it is. For instance, in one study value thinking was demonstrated to help people generate a *more extensive*, and *better organized*, set of decision options than alternative thinking (León, 1999). It leads people to "come up with alternatives that are more innovative," says Orfelio León, author of the study. And under circumstances where value thinking leads to the generation of fewer options, as it did in a second study, they are of *higher quality* than those produced by alternative thinking (Selart and Johansen, 2011). They are "more innovative and insightful in that they were more long term and visionary," note Marcus Selart and Svein Tvedt Johansen, coauthors of that study.

Value thinking is therefore not so much about generating *more* alternatives, though that might sometimes be an outcome. Rather, says Keeney, it "creates better alternatives." These alternatives are better because they get to the heart of *what you care about* in relation to the decision you are making.

The first step in value thinking, then, is to think about what you care about in a particular decision situation. Call this step defining objectives or goals. The second step is to apply what Keeney calls the "Why Is That Important?" test, or WITI, to each objective. This helps you determine whether a particular objective is itself fundamental or a means to a more fundamental objective. Consider the following example concerning environmental issues, based on Keeney's 1994 *Sloan Management Review* paper.

Suppose you have the task of transporting hazardous material for disposal. What is a fundamental objective here? Minimizing the distance traveled so as to reduce the chances of an accident sounds like a good goal. But that might route you through urban environments, potentially risking a lot of people to exposure to hazardous material. Cutting down on the risk of accidents is obviously laudable, but the overriding goal that emerges is to keep harm to citizens to a minimum. You can ask, Why is that important? The answer? It is simply important. You have now found a fundamental objective in this decision situation.

The rationale for going through this process is to discover the importance of each objective you come up with and to see how each relates to the others on your list. "Using [this process] to stimulate thought about how to get to what you care about makes good sense," says Keeney. "It makes much better sense than trying to get what you care about without thoroughly understanding what it is you care about."

Value Thinking in Retirement Planning

When you are planning the landscape of your retirement future, I am certain you will want it to fully reflect what you care about. And what you care about is likely to involve more than just one goal. The thinking tool for this first stage in planning for your retirement future therefore fully embraces the principle and process of value thinking.

Your first task, then, is to pause, step back, and ask yourself the following questions about your retirement future:

What do I care about?

What are my goals and values?

What matters most to me?

You will come up with your own objectives, of course. That is the point of the exercise: to allow each individual to discover his or her own values rather than having values imposed on them by someone else.

By way of example, here are some espoused goals we heard while developing this first step of the GPS process:

Some of "Allan"'s* goals:

"Take care of the kids

I'd like to travel

Donate to charity

Do volunteer work in the community"

Some of "Jennifer"'s goals:

"Have an after-tax income of $350,000

Have a second home, preferably on Nantucket

Enjoy a healthy life

Work with charities"

This is what "Richard" said: "I'd like to have enough money so that my wife and I can enjoy our retirement together."

We told Richard that his goal was laudable and understandable but too broad for the GPS exercise. We encouraged him to be more specific, just as Allan and Jennifer had been.

---

* Names of respondents have been changed but the content has not.

We encourage you to do the same. This more reflective process helps you begin to discover who you really are and what is really important to you. Gradually you will begin to assemble in your mind a set of goals that really matter to you in your retirement years.

This is what you do:

STEP 1: Take a blank piece of paper and carefully list all of the goals you have for your retirement future. Take as much time as you need.

You have now completed the first of seven steps in planning for your retirement future using the GPS process.

■

The next chapter in the GPS process, Step 2, Discover Blind Spots, addresses the challenge of coming up with a complete list of the alternatives that are important to you.

REFERENCES

Keeney, Ralph L. 1992a. *Value-Focused Thinking: A path to creative decision making.* Cambridge, MA: Harvard University Press.
Keeney, Ralph L. 1992b. Op. cit. p viii.
Keeney, Ralph L. 1992c. Op. cit. p 24.

Keeney, Ralph L. 2004. "Making Better Decision Makers."
    Decision Analysis 1, no. 4: 193–204.
León, Orfelio G. 1999. "Value-Focused Thinking Versus
    Alternative-Focused Thinking: Effects on Generation of
    Objectives." *Organizational Behavior and Human Decision
    Processes* 80, no. 3: 213–227.
Selart, Marcus, and Svein T. Johansen. 2011. "Understand-
    ing the Role of Value-Focused Thinking in Idea Man-
    agement." *Creativity and Innovation Management* 20, no.
    3: 196–206.

STEP 2

Discover Blind Spots

Buying a house is one of the biggest decisions any of us makes in our lifetime. There are so many things to consider. Imagine that you and your partner are on the verge of signing papers on a house and you are delighted with the one you've chosen. It has everything you are looking for in the ideal home. It's in a desirable neighborhood. It's the perfect size for you right now—three bedrooms, two bathrooms, and a rec room. The garden is big but not so big as to be unmanageable, and it's planted with low-maintenance ground cover and bushes. What more could you want?

A lot more, probably. How is the commute to both of your jobs? Is public transportation nearby? What about the nearest supermarket? Can you walk to a decent restaurant? You don't have kids right now, but suppose you do. Would the local school match the standards you want for their education? And are three bedrooms really adequate, especially when the second child comes along? Where would Grandma stay? Perhaps you should have thought about the possibility of a granny suite, too?

Are you still ready to sign those papers?

Behavioral Challenge:
Thinking Blind Spots

In a 2008 paper on decision making (Bond, Carlson, and Keeney, 2008), Ralph Keeney and two colleagues cited the following apt quote by the German philosopher Friedrich Nietzsche, which he wrote in 1879:

> Forgetting our objectives is the most frequent stupidity in which we indulge ourselves.

Although he was perhaps a little ungenerous to use the term "stupidity" in this context, Nietzsche nevertheless put his finger on the behavioral challenge we face when we try to bring to mind *all* the goals relevant to a decision before us. You might imagine, reasonably I would say, that if you've gone through the process of value thinking for a particular decision, as we saw in the previous step, Identify Your Goals, that you would end up with a comprehensive list of goals.

You will remember, however, that the aim of value thinking is not only to increase the range of goals that come to mind but also to ensure that you come up with better goals, ones that reflect what you care about. "OK," you might now say, "even if I didn't come up with a full list of relevant goals for this decision, at least I got all the ones that are important to me. Right?" Remarkably, the answer is "No, you probably did not." The reason is that all of us are susceptible to what we might call "thinking blind spots."

Consider the outcome of a 2008 study of a group of first-year MBA students who had not yet selected an organization where they were going to do an upcoming summer internship (Bond, Carlson, and Keeney, 2008).

The students were asked the following question:

> What objectives are relevant to you when selecting from potential opportunities for your summer internship?

The objectives could include items such as "helps me make good networking contacts," "lets me work with a diverse group of people," "is challenging," and so on. The students were given a week to ruminate on the above question and were encouraged to talk it over with other students or whomever they believed might give helpful input. They then had to email a list of objectives to the study's authors. So, no time pressure, no restrictions. Most students came up with around seven objectives.

Now, here you have a group of bright individuals, presumably serious about their studies and their future, who had a lot of time to think about the question before them. You would expect them to do a reasonably competent job of bringing to mind the objectives that were most important to them. And even if they overlooked an objective here and there, you would expect those to be of rather-limited importance. Wouldn't you?

Meanwhile, the study's authors put together what they called a "master list" of objectives, twenty-nine in all, garnered partly from the participants' own lists and from brainstorming around the question. (As you can see, there is no "magic" about a master list, despite its power. It is simply a structured assembly of all available information.) The students were then shown the master list and asked to do two things:

1. Identify objectives on the master list that you now recognize should have been on your own self-generated lists but were in fact absent.
2. Rank the recognized objectives in importance relative to your self-generated objectives.

You would, I think, find the outcome rather shocking, except of course that I've pretty much telegraphed what it was. On average, the students had about seven self-generated objectives and almost eight recognized objectives that they didn't think of when given a week and a lot of opportunity to do so. Moreover, the students ranked the recognized objectives as being of almost equal importance as the objectives they came up with themselves. These recognized objectives are the students' thinking blind spots.

To summarize this important result: When asked to generate a comprehensive list of objectives that were important to them, these bright, motivated students came up with barely half the number of objectives that they ultimately acknowledged should be on the list. And the ones that they had initially omitted were judged to be just about as important as the ones on the initial lists.

Why this striking failure? In a second paper, the authors of the above study asked the students why they thought their own self-generated list had been deficient (Bond, Carlson, and Keeney, 2010). About a third said their thinking had been too shallow, such as due to a "lack of thought" and "not thinking it through." At the same time, almost half of the students believed their list had been deficient because they were thinking too narrowly and "got too focused and closed my mind around only a few things." The authors of the study therefore concluded that "the generation of decision objectives is often hindered by cognitive processing that is insufficient in both depth and breadth."

The findings by these authors are consistent with a great deal of literature on how we store items in memory (often in categories, for example) and the challenge of recalling such items (failure to jump between categories). The upshot of all this research is that we should not be at all surprised that, even when we try hard, recalling items from our memory banks will be spotty at best, with only a few memories coming to mind at any particular time. And we often do not work as hard at recalling items from memory as we should. Attempting to recall everything that is relevant and important to a particular decision is extremely difficult and we often need help.

Going back to the decision you and your partner are making: signing the papers on that house. You probably did think of some of the additional factors I mentioned, such as the local transportation, shopping and dining-out facilities, schools, and so on. But you know now that, no matter how vigorously you apply your mind to the task, the list of factors you self-generate and judge to be relevant and important in your choice of house is likely to be less than complete. I know it's hard to believe, given how momentous such a decision is and how hard you might try, but, as you've seen, thinking blind spots will almost certainly trip you up.

In Step 1, Identify Your Goals, the cause of the thinking trap was fast thinking, focusing too quickly on what is in front of us. In this case it is different. "To the extent that contemplation of one's objectives involves a substantial amount of reasoned deliberation (alignment of personal values to attributes of the decision, consideration of alternative outcomes, etc.)," say the study's authors, "narrow and shallow thinking may be viewed as deficiencies in [deliberation]" (Bond, Carlson, and Keeney, 2010).

Our slow, deliberative thinking process, which is often quite reliable, suffers from laziness and, in this case, obviously needs help in dealing with thinking blind spots.

Behavioral Solution: The Master List

You will have noticed, I'm sure, that the behavioral solution and thinking tool in this case are contained in the study I just described. It is the master list. Whenever you face a decision of significant complexity you will greatly benefit from compiling a master list of all relevant objectives or goals, using other resources that may be available. You could, for instance, compare notes with others who face the same decision and merge your list with theirs or consult experts for their input.

For example, suppose you need to evaluate options to adjust your diet for wellness or health considerations. You might ask one or two doctors for advice, and they might tell you that your goals should include minimizing catastrophic risks such as stroke or cardiovascular issues (through lowering cholesterol intake or increasing fiber intake, for example). You could also ask your family members, and they might say that goals should include minimizing chronic issues stemming from excessive weight (such as risk of diabetes). You might ask your friends, and they might indicate that goals should include social aspects, such as being able to have occasional fun when eating with friends or spending time with a spouse when preparing or eating food. You might also do some Web research that indicates that dieting goals should be pragmatic and that options need to be relatively convenient, affordable, and easy. And don't forget to think for yourself—shouldn't flavor and enjoyment matter, too?

The basic idea for developing a master list of goals is that you want to get as much input as you can by asking for advice from people you know, talking to experts, doing research and the like. Merge the lists together, reduce some overlap, and voilà! You now have a master list of possible goals to think about for changing your diet and improving your health.

The key lesson here is that when you are faced with the task of assembling a comprehensive list of goals relevant to an important decision, having a master list of goals is a powerful tool to aid in the process. This applies to many decisions, such as figuring out where to live, buying a house, deciding between job offers, and planning for retirement.

Using the Master List for Retirement Planning

I'm certain that when you plan for your retirement, you will want to be sure that the goals you come up with not only reflect your values but also cover *everything* that is important to you. I'm also certain that when you generate your list of goals for your retirement, as you just did using value thinking, you will be confident that you have covered all important bases. But, as you now know, almost certainly you will be wrong. You, too, will have thinking blind spots and need help in your decision making. It's likely that I would need help, too.

The thinking tool here is based on the power of the master list to help you identify important goals that don't readily come to mind—the blind spots in your thinking. We worked diligently with dozens of financial advisers and hundreds of individuals to develop a master list of twelve retirement goals that we believe is as close to being comprehensive as can be practically achieved and covers almost everyone's needs. Please note that there is no implied ranking of importance in the structure of this list.

Financial independence: Knowing I can pay my basic expenses for as long as I live and not become a burden on my kids.

Healthcare: Being able to pay for my medical expenses for as long as I live.

Housing: Choosing my own living situation, such as staying in my home, buying a second home, or downsizing.

Travel and leisure: Taking trips and doing fun activities.

Lifestyle: Maintaining my current, or a better, lifestyle.

Second career: Beginning a new career, starting a business, or working on my own terms.

Self-improvement: Investing in personal growth, such as taking classes and learning new skills.

Family bequests: Leaving money to my family and doing so with minimal taxes and hassles.

Giving back: Contributing to causes important to me with my time and/or my money.

Social engagement: Enjoying the company of friends and family and not feeling lonely.

Ending life with dignity: Preparing to experience my last days my way.

Control: Feeling I still "drive" my own life.

You will have some kind of reaction to the master list, I'm sure. When we were developing this second step of the GPS process, we heard a lot of positive feedback about the master list concept from both financial advisers and people approaching retirement. Here are some of their comments. How do they compare with yours?

"It would have been easier if I had had the master list to begin with."

"On the master list, it's good to have some goals that are not directly related to finances. The only things I addressed were financial."

"The master list has goals you don't typically see, such as ending life with dignity, self-improvement. I like that."

Now it is your opportunity to go through the exercise with the master list.

There are two parts to this thinking tool.

STEP 2A: Put aside the list of goals you self-generated in Step 1. Turn it upside down and behave as if it doesn't exist. Now review the master list of twelve retirement goals above and identify the ones you believe are most important to you.

STEP 2B: Now refer to the original list of goals you generated in Step 1. Identify all the goals that you selected from the master list that do not appear on your original self-generated list. These are your retirement goal "blind spots."

You now have a comprehensive list of retirement goals that is tailored to your own particular needs and what you care about.

■

Now that you have a comprehensive list of retirement goals, your next challenge in the GPS process, Step 3, is to figure out what you care about most and what you care about least. In other words, you will face the task of prioritizing your goals.

REFERENCES

Bond, Samuel D., Kurt A. Carlson, and Ralph L. Keeney. 2008. "Generating Objectives: Can Decision Makers Articulate What They Want?" *Management Science* 54, no. 1: 56–70.
Bond, Samuel D., Kurt A. Carlson, and Ralph L. Keeney. 2010. "Improving the Generation of Decision Objectives." *Decision Analysis* 7, no. 3: 238–255.

STEP 3

Prioritize Your Goals

Here's a hypothetical exercise. Robert is director of healthcare management at a major hospital and he faces what in technical parlance is referred to as a "resource allocation decision." Sounds like a straightforward logical problem, doesn't it? Put the resources where they will generate the most benefit. However, Robert's decision is complicated because it has a human face to it.

Johnny is a very sick five-year-old. He needs a liver transplant, which is an expensive procedure. Giving Johnny the organ he needs will consume the $1 million that Robert has available for discretionary spending this quarter. Without the transplant, Johnny will die in the very near future. At the same time, Robert could allocate that $1 million to urgent needs in the hospital, such as replacing outdated diagnostic equipment.

What decision do you think Robert should make? You probably have a fairly strong opinion about that, don't you? More to the point, How would you feel if you were in Robert's shoes, facing this decision? You would probably feel very uncomfortable, maybe even anxious and stressed.

Hold that thought as we first explore the behavioral

challenge that Robert faces with this decision, which is making a trade-off between Johnny's life and hospital improvements, and then we will return to Robert's situation in more detail later in this step.

Behavioral Challenge:
Making Trade-offs

Making trade-offs is part of everyday life and most of the time we take them in stride. But some trade-offs cause real anguish and there is considerable literature on the different forms of difficult trade-offs and the psychological impact of being unable to avoid them. For instance, in a study by Dutch social psychologist Frenk van Harreveld and others, students who were forced to prioritize and make choices reported feeling more uncomfortable to the point of physically breaking out in a sweat than those who did not have to prioritize and choose (Harreveld et al., 2009).

One of my favorite examples of trade-offs concerns time. We often hear people, ourselves included, say, "I don't have time for this or that." But we all have the same amount of time available to us, don't we, whether we are the president of the United States or an average working person. We all have twenty-four hours a day and seven days a week. The issue is not that we don't have time, it's how we elect to make use of the time we have available to us. We don't have time to do everything we might want to do, so we have to prioritize, we have to make trade-offs.

Consider this uncomfortable time trade-off. You are the parent of a thirteen-year-old girl, Rachel, who is a soccer fanatic and something of a rising star on her school soccer team. Naturally, Rachel wants you to watch at least some of her practice games and be present at all of her competitive games, usually on Saturday mornings. At the same time, you are a rising star in your law firm and on the verge of making partner. The culture of the firm is typical of most law firms: You have to be in the office at all hours to demonstrate your commitment to the job and to show you are partner material. You know that if you go to Rachel's competitive games on Saturday mornings you are jeopardizing your chances of making partner by not being in the office. You also know that if you don't go to the games you are jeopardizing your relationship with Rachel. You have to make a choice about which is more important to you. I'm sure many of you are familiar with some version of this painful time trade-off.

When we face difficult decisions, we automatically look for ways to avoid them. Failing that, we can try to make these decisions easier, but this can lead to a costly trade-off. For instance, when a difficult decision is unavoidable, we sometimes use a technique called "elimination by aspects," which strips away some of the complexity of the situation and makes the decision easier (Tversky, 1972).

For example, imagine the following. You are taking a summer vacation in Greece with your spouse, starting in Athens. You need to book flights and you know there are multiple options to consider: different airlines, nonstop or multiple connections, vacation packages, date-sensitive pricing, and more. And you are busy. Maybe you could simplify the task by narrowing your search to your favorite airlines. Easy. Done. Of course, the trade-off might be that you miss a terrific discount fare on an airline that's not on your list. That's the price you pay for making a difficult task easier.

Let's go back to Robert and his difficult and emotion-laden decision. University of Pennsylvania psychologist Philip

Tetlock has labeled the situation Robert faces—saving Johnny or improving the hospital—a "taboo trade-off" (Tetlock et al., 2000). Many people find it morally or ethically repulsive to put a dollar value on someone's life. Hence the term "taboo trade-off." Going against a taboo is the equivalent of violating a sacred principle and doing so can cause moral outrage. For example, when a group of students were asked in a hypothetical exercise their reaction to Robert's having decided to improve the hospital instead of having saved Johnny's life, they recorded a moral outrage level of 5.14 (on a scale of 1 to 7). Robert was breaking a sacred principle, a taboo.

Even more striking is what happens when Robert is said to take a considerable amount of time before deciding that improving hospital facilities is more important. Now, you would expect that the students would want Robert to weigh the options carefully and take his time before coming to a decision. But no, they are even more outraged in this case, registering 5.71 on the outrage scale. With taboo trade-offs, people want you to "do the right thing" without even considering the other option.

Robert's story illustrates how some trade-offs can be extremely difficult and emotional. In this case the issues in play are not easily or directly comparable. How do you put a value on saving one life now versus enhancing treatment facilities, which may benefit many people over a longer period of time? But, because resources are limited, Robert cannot avoid making this challenging trade-off.

In colloquial terms, Robert may be said to have to choose between apples and oranges, because saving Johnny and improving the hospital are not directly comparable. Not that apples-to-apples trade-offs are necessarily easy on every occasion. Suppose, for example, improving hospital facilities was out of the picture and Robert had to choose between spending the $1 million to save Johnny or to save Jimmy, a second very sick five-year-old who also needs a liver transplant. Tetlock and his colleagues call this a "tragic trade-off."

Nevertheless, you can see how excruciatingly difficult Robert's taboo trade-off is when trying to do "the right thing" in this situation. As the authors of a 1998 article in *Harvard Business Review* put it, when you face trade-offs of this nature, "You're not just trading off apples and oranges; you're trading off apples and oranges and elephants" (Hammond, Keeney, and Raiffa, 1998). There's no comparison at all between a boy's life and the value of having new diagnostic medical equipment.

If you were in Robert's shoes, you would probably opt to save Johnny, wouldn't you? But would you want to be in Robert's shoes at that moment? Probably not. Most people wouldn't either, because we hate making trade-offs, especially emotionally difficult ones. The authors of that *Harvard Business Review* article suggest that, "Making wise trade-offs is one of the most important and difficult challenges in decision making." I totally agree.

The behavioral challenges at play when making choices or prioritizing could be twofold:

First, making trade-offs, which involves being analytical and deliberative, can demand substantial cognitive effort. We have a natural tendency to avoid doing that if we can. Daniel Kahneman, Nobel Prize laureate and behavioral economist, has this to say about deliberative thinking, in his book *Thinking, Fast and Slow:* "One of its main characteristics is laziness, a reluctance to invest more effort than is strictly necessary" (Kahneman, 2011).

Second, your emotions could be dragged into the process, making some trade-offs even more difficult.

The bottom line, then, is that not only does making trade-offs prove difficult and we hate making them but we even find making them annoying. So, what behavioral help is out there for these kinds of situations?

Behavioral Solution:
Employ a Prioritization Board

Unfortunately, behavioral solutions that help us overcome alternative thinking and blind spots elude us when making difficult trade-offs. Coming up with a good list of priorities is therefore a challenge and can be painful, no question about it. Having a guided process to help you do so, however, can make it more palatable.

A key to prioritizing is making sure that some things are designated as more important than others. Simply labeling everything as high priority is not prioritizing.

When prioritizing, it is also important to utilize a "budget constraint" and recognize that resources are limited, potentially even scarce. The resource constraint could be dollars, time, number of items, or many other options. In the case of Robert, he was forced to prioritize with a budget constraint of $1 million that could only be used for one option or the other.

There are many ways to implement a prioritization system. In some cases, a simple ranking method might work when the number of options is relatively small. For example, imagine there are only three viable candidates to be hired for a job. As the employer, you might prioritize which person you offer the job to first, going to the second and then third candidates only if negotiations with the prior candidate fall through.

But a ranking task can become more difficult when the number of items to prioritize gets bigger. In this case a good prioritization system (as we'll see with our retirement application) is to sort items into buckets based on what you consider to be most important, moderately important, or least important. A budget constraint could limit the number of items per bucket.

The Prioritization Board in Retirement Planning

You have now reached the point in the GPS process where you have created your own comprehensive list of retirement goals. These might include social engagement, ability to cope with healthcare costs, giving back to society, self-improvement, and so on. You are definitely looking at apples and oranges and elephants now, aren't you? What retirement goals are most important to you and how do you make trade-offs among them?

If you had unlimited material resources, you wouldn't have to make choices or weigh the relative importance you place on different goals. You could indeed have it all. More likely, however, you face what Robert faced: the need to make tough choices because your resources are limited. As a result, you need to go through a prioritization exercise.

In our exercise, there is a maximum of twelve retirement goals on the master list. However, we felt that the task of ranking the goals from 1 to 12 might well be excessively difficult, as the difference between say the eighth- and ninth-ranked goals could be tough to distinguish. Therefore, we settled on a prioritization board that has three buckets, namely goals of most importance, goals of moderate importance, and goals of least importance, as described earlier. A workable grouping seemed to be three goals in the most-important level, four goals in the moderate level, and five goals in the least-important level. Structured like this, you should be able to appreciate the range of importance across all the goals. You also should be able to recognize the budget constraint, as you have fewer goals in the most-important bucket than in the other two buckets.

For this exercise, you will need to establish your own prioritization board either by using the Goal Planning System app or by printing out a paper version of it by going to the "Additional Information and Support" section at http://www.retirementgoalplanningsystem.com.

Now, using your prioritization board, consider the following steps:

STEP 3A: Look at your collection of goals for retirement, think carefully, and identify *the single-most-important goal*. Now think carefully again and identify *the single-least-important goal*.

Take your time and consider these decisions carefully. When you are ready, place your most-important goal on the top level of the prioritization board and your least-important one on the bottom level. By doing this you have created a range of importance among your retirement goals.

STEP 3B: Next, review your remaining goals and, using the prioritization board, sort them into three categories, or buckets, according to how important they are to you: most important, moderately important, and least important. You may rearrange your goals as often as you need to until you are satisfied your priorities reflect your values.

You have now prioritized your retirement goals for the first time. Congratulations!

When we were developing this step in the GPS process and testing it with pre-retirees and financial advisers, we saw how challenging making trade-offs can be for some, just as we expected.

This comment by "Elaine," a pre-retiree, captures the anguish of making difficult trade-offs as well as the recognition of the need to do so:

> I did *not* like identifying the single-most-important goal and the single-least-important goal. I also *did not like* prioritizing the goals in between. I really wanted to label them *all* as most important. But I forced myself to do the exercise, and I have to admit that in the end I found it extremely valuable.

Here's what one financial adviser said on the same topic:

> I can see that prioritizing could be a painful exercise for a client, but I can also see the value in their doing it.

Making good decisions is the goal of the GPS. It doesn't, however, eliminate all the pain that is an inescapable element of the process. Having said that, I do believe that our guided prioritization process makes it far more manageable and that you will be glad you did.

■

What follows, a chapter called Steps 1–3 in Action, gives you an opportunity to follow the experiences of two people,

Francesca and Phillip, as they go through Steps 1–3 of the GPS exercise.

REFERENCES

Hammond, John S., Ralph L. Keeney, and Howard Raiffa. 1998. "Even Swaps: A Rational Method for Making Trade-Offs." *Harvard Business Review*, March-April: 3–11.

Harreveld, Frenk van, Bastiaan T. Rutjens, Mark Rotteveel, Loran F. Nordgren, and Joop van der Pligt. 2009. "Ambivalence and Decisional Conflict as a Cause of Psychological Discomfort: Feeling Tense Before Jumping off the Fence." *Journal of Experimental Social Psychology* 45, no. 1: 167–173.

Kahneman, Daniel. 2011. *Thinking, Fast and Slow*. New York: Farrar, Straus and Giroux.

Tversky, Amos. 1972. "Elimination by Aspects: A Theory of Choice." *Psychological Review* 79, no. 4: 281–299.

Tetlock, Philip E., Orie V. Kristel, S. Beth Elson, Jennifer S. Lerner, and Melanie C. Green. 2000. "The Psychology of the Unthinkable: Taboo Trade-Offs, Forbidden Base Rates, and Heretical Counterfactuals." *Journal of Personality and Social Psychology* 78, no. 5: 853–870.

Steps 1–3 in Action

Now, I have assured you along this journey that you are not alone in falling into the thinking traps you encountered in Steps 1 and 2, and I hope you believed me. But seeing is believing. In this step you will get a glimpse of two people who went through this same journey as part of the development of this book. You will see firsthand some of the limits on thinking that two smart and motivated individuals struggled with just as you almost certainly did. These stories are real but the names have been changed for anonymity.

The two people are Francesca and Phillip, to whom I briefly introduced you in the introduction. I won't telegraph what their separate experiences were—you will see that as you read on here—except to say that not only did they indeed struggle as you might have, but they also had quite different needs and goals in life, just as everyone does.

First, some background, beginning with Francesca.

Francesca is a successful executive in the financial services industry approaching her fiftieth birthday. And that is something of a surprise to her, her line of work, I mean. As a university undergraduate, Francesca was fascinated with languages and Middle Eastern studies. She fully expected to pursue this as a career and become an academic in this field of study. Instead, compelled by her "altruistic side," she started out working for an environmental agency, then went into the financial services sector (not enough money in altruism) and now works for a big company in New York City.

Francesca finds herself a little surprised to be in the big corporate world because it doesn't match who she feels she is at heart—a person who enjoys the outdoors, time alone, and giving back to society. She acknowledges that there are very real (material) benefits to being in the corporate world and feels fortunate that the work she wound up doing does indeed help people find financial stability in life. Nevertheless, as she approaches the Big Five-Oh, Francesca is beginning to feel that her work life (long hours in the office, twenty hours commuting each week, endless meetings, the inevitable bureaucracy), fulfilling though it is, is "not enough."

On top of this, a serious health scare a couple of years ago made Francesca realize she should be doing what is important to her—now, or at least as soon as possible.

These are Francesca's self-identified goals in the order she selected them, which she arrived at through Step 1 of the GPS exercise:

♦ Giving back—altruistic activities
♦ Doing something new—a different kind of work
♦ Health—being healthy and staying healthy
♦ Healthcare—making sure I've got good coverage for my husband and me
♦ Leaving money to causes I care about
♦ Spending more time with people I care about
♦ Travel
♦ Move to a place to which I feel more connected

Francesca then consulted the master list of retirement goals, Step 2, and selected the following, in this order:

- ◆ Financial independence
- ◆ Healthcare
- ◆ Housing
- ◆ Travel and leisure
- ◆ Second career
- ◆ Self-improvement
- ◆ Giving back
- ◆ Social engagement
- ◆ Ending life with dignity

Notice something remarkable? Right at the top of Francesca's Step 2 list is financial independence, something she realized is important to her when she perused the master list, yet this goal was absent from the list she made in Step 1.

Now, Francesca is a good friend, and we have spoken often over the past year about the GPS as it was being developed. She was therefore familiar with how the system works and what goals appear on the master list. Yet when she did the exercise and looked at the master list to see if there was something she had missed, she discovered she had missed something extremely important to her. "When I saw those two words—financial independence—under the master list of goals, I realized I don't want to be dependent on anybody," she said. "How could I have missed that in Step 1?"

So that was a big surprise. Here was someone who was as familiar with the GPS exercise as anyone could be, without actually having done it, but something that she acknowledged as being extremely important to her had simply not come to mind when she was initially putting together her list of goals. That was a huge thinking blind spot for Francesca. This is a salutary lesson for all of us.

Another goal on the master list that was absent from Francesca's initial list but cropped up when prompted by the master list was ending life with dignity. We know very well that for many people, thinking about death and dying is discomforting, which makes planning for the years leading up to that inevitable event difficult. We need prompting to think constructively about this important eventuality.

After Francesca had completed Step 3, Prioritize Your Goals, she said the experience had been "very, very difficult because a lot of things seemed to be important." Francesca is not alone. Most people find prioritization a tough challenge. At the same time, most people say they are grateful for the outcome, once they force themselves to do the exercise.

In any case, here's her prioritized list:

- ◆ Most important: Financial independence, giving back, healthcare
- ◆ Moderately important: Housing, self-improvement, second career, ending life with dignity
- ◆ Least important: Social engagement, travel and leisure

Notice that one of the three most important goals—financial independence—had not even been on Francesca's initial list of goals. And ending life with dignity, which had also been absent from her initial list, was now judged to be moderately important.

■

So that was Francesca's story. Now it's time to hear Phillip's story.

Phillip is a professor at a top university in the Northeast; he is nearing seventy and his generous salary has enabled him to save adequately for retirement, so he could retire if he chose but hasn't so far. Like Francesca, Phillip is more than a little surprised to find himself where he is now in his career. His first love had been history and that's where he had expected his future to take him. Phillip's passion for studying history manifested itself at a young age. He remembers, for instance, as a boy in junior high riding three miles on his bike to spend hours in the city library, reading Edward Gibbon's *The History of the Decline and Fall of the Roman Empire*, which, Phillip tells me, is a classic work, originally published in six volumes, beginning in 1776. Not your usual teenage reading. Instead of following his heart, however, Phillip found himself becoming an academic economist and has had—and is still having—a distinguished career in studying the efficiency of markets.

Phillip has been married to Joanna for thirty years and the two are devoted to each other. They are their own best friends. Phillip has traveled throughout his adult life, often in company with Joanna, pursuing his busy career. Virtually all of his vacation travel has been tagged onto a business trip, an arrangement that appeals to his Baptist frugality.

A couple of years before Phillip completed the GPS exercise, Joanna had a freak skiing accident that, they both recognized to their horror, could have ended her life. It was a life-changing experience.

Before detailing Phillip's results for Step 1 of the GPS exercise, I'd like to point out what you have probably already noticed.

Here are two people, Francesca and Phillip, with one focus: namely, contemplating what will be important to them in their retirement years. But see how very different they are, in age, interests, preferences, and dreams. These little vignettes underscore that we are all different, in many ways, and this will influence what we believe will be important to us in our different futures.

Notice, too, that they both encountered life-threatening scares, Francesca to her own life, Phillip to his wife's. It's a reminder that many unknowns lie ahead for all of us, risks that could dramatically affect even the best-laid plans. And Francesca has the additional risk of living many, many years after she retires, if she were to do so very early. Being able to sustain oneself financially over a long time is a challenge.

Here are Phillip's self-identified goals, which he generated in Step 1:

♦ Happy retirement with my wife
♦ Financial independence
♦ Travel
♦ Maintain health

When Phillip was talking about his future goals, he made it clear that he was really thinking about goals for himself and Joanna, shared goals *as a couple*. Phillip makes a good point, because most couples who are entering retirement want to remain together during retirement. Couples who elect to go through the GPS exercise should therefore give some thought as to how to balance their goals and needs as individuals with their collective goals and needs as a couple. One way to do this would be for spouses to do the exercises separately and then compare notes. In the best of all possible worlds, the outcomes would be very similar. But if there are striking differences, better to know about them before entering retirement, when there is an opportunity to talk about and resolve them rather than during retirement, when they might become a source of discord.

In Step 2 of the GPS exercise, Discover Blind Spots, Phillip consulted the master list of retirement goals. These are the goals he selected from that master list:

♦ Financial independence
♦ Travel
♦ Healthcare
♦ Family bequests
♦ Ending life with dignity

Phillip's thinking blind spots were family bequests and ending life with dignity. About the latter he said, "I have had the experience of family who have gone through aspects of dementia, assisted living, and so forth. So these are things that are salient to me at my age, whereas they wouldn't have been when I was in my fifties." As you can see, ending life with dignity is important to Phillip, yet somehow it simply did not come to mind when he was trying to think of all the things he would value in retirement. The master list provides a means of broadening your thinking so you can look at it and say, "Oh, yes, that too. I should have thought of it in the first place!"

Phillip produced the following prioritized list of goals by going through the challenging trade-off process prompted by Step 3:

♦ Most important: financial independence, travel
♦ Moderately important: family bequest, ending life with dignity
♦ Least important: healthcare

Notice that for Phillip, two of the moderately important goals—family bequest and ending life with dignity—weren't on his initial list of self-identified goals.

Also notice that, although there is some overlap between Francesca's and Phillip's prioritized lists, for the most part they are quite different. Again, this reflects individual tastes and preferences and the need for each of us to pay close attention to our own tastes and preferences. They define who we are and where we want to go. The GPS exercise enables you to discover this.

■

You can stop the GPS exercise right here if you so choose, at the end of Step 3, the prioritization process. After all, you now have prioritized a list of goals for retirement, something you likely did not have at the outset. However, the second section of this book—Steps 4 to 7—offers an opportunity to go deeper in your thinking with the objective of generating an even-more-thoughtful list of priorities for your retirement years. I therefore urge you to continue. And you will again have the opportunity of observing how Francesca and Phillip fared in the exercise.

Think Beyond One Future

Mimi was a housewife in the San Fernando Valley, in southwestern California, when, at age fifty-five, she discovered that her husband was unfaithful to her. Being a feisty woman, she would have none of it, packed her bags, and left him to begin a better life on her own.

Like many women in her situation, however, Mimi struggled financially. Things went from bad to worse and before long Mimi was living on the streets of Los Angeles, homeless. The day-to-day life of the homeless is tough, obviously, and the prospects even worse. The average life expectancy of homeless people, for instance, is between forty-two and fifty-two years of age (O'Connell, 2005). Mimi was older than that when she joined their ranks, of course, but she was clearly in for a challenging future.

That was thirty-five years ago. So what would your prediction be for Mimi, after all this time has passed? Is she still homeless? Is she even still with us?

Behavioral Challenge: One Future?

In pondering this prediction exercise you probably do what most people do, which is latch onto a likely outcome and fixate on it. It's a tendency that Duke University psychologist John Payne describes as a "focus on one future." In this case, you probably would say that Mimi almost certainly passed away many years ago.

Here's what actually happened.

One rainy night almost twenty years ago, the owner of Fox Laundry, on Santa Monica Boulevard, took pity on Mimi and allowed her to stay in the laundry overnight. One night stretched to eighteen years, with Mimi volunteering in the laundry by day, sleeping there at night, and relying on tips from customers to buy food.

During this time she happened to meet the zany, bearded comic Zack Galifianakis. They became friends for a while, but then she saw nothing of him for years. Meanwhile, the actor-director Yaniv Rokah noticed Mimi waking up in the laundry early one morning and started talking with her. Rokah became entranced with Mimi's life story and decided to raise money to do a documentary on her life, titled *Queen Mimi*. It was released in 2014.*

A couple of years ago, Mimi fell on hard times again. Galifianakis got word of Mimi's plight and wanted to help his erstwhile friend. He bought an apartment for Mimi near the laundry and recruited his friend Renee Zellweger

---

* As an aside, I was drawn into Mimi's story, too, and wound up being the executive producer of the film. I believe her story highlights the need to think about our uncertain world and its multiple possible futures. Hopefully, the movie will succeed in delivering the message to many people.

to help furnish it as well as to keep the refrigerator well stocked with food. Friendships developed all around and before long, Mimi was walking arm in arm with Galifianakis down Hollywood's red carpets at film premieres, most recently of *The Hangover Part III* (Goldberg, 2014).

Oscar Wilde once said, "We are all in the gutter, but some of us are looking at the stars." And Queen Mimi recently said, "Life is too much fun."

I guess Mimi is one of the stargazers. What a woman!

The lesson of Mimi's remarkable story is that we are not very good at making predictions and typically overlook unlikely outcomes, bad and good. There is more chance in life than we generally think about. Remember, since there are a lot of different unlikely outcomes, one of those unlikely outcomes could easily take place. In this case, the unlikely outcome was that Mimi would not only survive but also thrive.

Here's a case of poor prediction: the recent situation with oversupply of crude oil in the United States, aided in part by new drilling techniques. As some headlines have proclaimed, we are literally "drowning in oil." In the decades since the 1970s and 1980s, when strict export restrictions were put in place and when cutoffs of Middle Eastern oil supply were characterized as grave national security threats (Myre, 2014), the situation has completely turned around. As of 2013, the United States now meets 86 percent of its energy needs from its own domestic supply, the highest level since 1986 (Efstathiou, 2014). Some are now forecasting that in the near future we will overtake Russia and Saudi Arabia as the world's largest producer of oil. Who would have predicted this?

Another example is a personal story of narrow thinking in prediction. Twenty years ago I was offered an investment opportunity in an international coffee shop chain, when it was still very small. Being the coffee snob that I am, I thought to myself, "Why would anybody pay four bucks for not very good coffee served in a paper cup, you don't even get a spoon, and the place has no atmosphere?" My answer was that nobody would. I thought it was the dumbest idea on the planet. Today that company has many thousands of outlets around the world and billions of dollars in annual revenues. When I thought about the future of what I considered to not be a very promising operation, I focused on only one possibility, failure. I couldn't see how success was even remotely possible. Didn't even think about it. I guess I wasn't thinking broadly enough.

The stories of Mimi, the U.S. crude oil boom, and my shortsighted investment decision in a coffee shop venture illustrate the tendency to think too narrowly about outcomes. We quickly come up with one future, the one we believe to be most likely, and fail to appreciate that there are many possible futures. We cannot know which of those possible futures is going to happen, but we should at least be aware of them and acknowledge the possibility that something we think is extremely unlikely might come to pass.

The behavioral challenge, then, is our tendency to be seduced by one future when making predictions. What we need to do is to think beyond one future, reflecting on the fact that the world is an uncertain place.

Behavioral Solution: Employ Prospective Hindsight

Humans are, as I just said, generally rather poor about recognizing and predicting an uncertain future. By contrast, we are rather good about coming up with stories to explain how a particular event might have transpired. Humans, after all, are born storytellers. We love to make sense of our environment and what happens around us. It's in our genes, you might say.

Some years back Deborah Mitchell, J. Edward Russo, and Nancy Pennington explored the basis for a thinking tool that exploits this natural storytelling ability. Called Prospective Hindsight, the strategy itself is simple: Instead of trying to predict possible future events, we should try to explain events *as if they had already happened* (Mitchell, Russo, and Pennington, 1989). The idea is that instead of predicting the uncertain future, you imagine that an event in the future has certainly happened and then come up with stories that explain how the event occurred. This technique expands your thinking and imagination.

"Prospective hindsight may help in intuitive forecasting by utilizing people's natural facility to generate event chains for sure outcomes," write Mitchell and her colleagues. "In this way they can increase realistic awareness of . . . the range of potential outcomes." In other words, this thinking tool should open the imagination to a greater range of possibilities.

The authors measured the effect of prospective hindsight in the following way. They divided study participants into two groups, both of which were given the following scenario:

> Heather, a good friend of yours at work, has decided she will throw a large dinner party, including colleagues from work. She is anxious to make the party a huge success and has spared no expense in putting it on.

One group of participants was told the following:

> As it will turn out, the party will be a great success. Please list as many reasons as you can think of why the party will be a great success.

The second group was asked to do the following:

> Please list as many reasons as you can think of why the party may be a great success.

In other words, the first group was told to assume that the party certainly *will* be a great success and to explain why. The second group was tasked with predicting why the party *may be* a success; therefore, there was an essence of uncertainty for that group. You can see that the people in the first group were asked to apply prospective hindsight in generating their stories. The upshot was that they came up with 30 percent more reasons to explain why the party would indeed be a success than those who were in prediction mode. In a similar case the disparity was nearly as high as 70 percent. It is apparent that prospective hindsight is indeed a powerful thinking tool in expanding one's imagination.

Let's go back to my investment opportunity in a fledgling coffee shop venture. You will recall that I very quickly decided that I wasn't going to waste my money on a business model that, I reasoned, didn't have the slimmest chance of success. Done. I didn't even consider alternatives. Had I gone through a prospective hindsight exercise, I might have considered more possibilities for the outcome of the venture.

While I initially could only see the coffee venture as a failure, if I had gone through a prospective hindsight

exercise I might have also thought: "Suppose it is a spectac-
ular success, eventually becoming a multibillion-dollar
international company. How could that happen?" If I had
thought it through, I might have come up with a lot of reasons. Globalization was a big deal at the time. Businesses
were just starting to go into China and elsewhere. People
traveling the world wanted coffee with safe-to-drink milk,
which was not always available at the time. Where would
you have gone to get your coffee? Well, you might go to
that international coffee chain you are so familiar with.
Maybe the company will be able to sell a cappuccino for
four bucks, even in India and China. Other reasons for this
coffee shop's success may be that familiarity is more important to customers than a congenial coffee shop experience or
great coffee. It could also be attributed to a well-crafted
marketing message or the leadership talents of its charis-
matic CEO.

As it turns out, it's easy to come up with a success story
for this company. Had I explored these possible futures
earlier, maybe I would have invested in the company and
even if I still hadn't, I would have at least expanded my
thinking.

Using Prospective Hindsight
in Retirement Planning

There are many risks and uncertainties in retirement, such
as how well your investments will fare in the markets,
whether health problems put unexpected demands on your
financial resources, the possibility of future cognitive
impairment, and how long you are going to live. We can't
know what will happen to us in the future, but we need to

expand our thinking beyond one future to explore a range of retirement possibilities.

Here's how you use the prospective hindsight thinking tool to do that:

STEP 4A: Imagine your retirement if things went well. Imagine it is twenty years from now. What would your life have been like? How would you describe this situation in terms of your goals?

Take a few minutes to describe what your life would have been like. You can do this verbally with your adviser or spouse or write down what comes to mind.

STEP 4B: Imagine your retirement if things went badly. Now imagine it's twenty years from now and things went badly. What would your life have been like? How would you describe this situation in terms of your goals?

Take a few minutes to describe verbally or in writing what your life would have been like in this scenario.

You don't have a specific action to take at this point. Simply let the emotions and thoughts that are provoked by this exercise percolate in your mind.

In our experience with testing the prospective hindsight exercise with individuals, we found that the "if things go badly" scenario had an especially profound influence on how people wanted their future to be. For one individual, "Anthony," who was one of the first financial advisers to do the exercise, the experience was quite moving.

As with many people who contemplate bad retirement outcomes during the exercise, Anthony very quickly recognized that losing social interactions—being lonely—would be scary and painful. But Anthony was specifically concerned that, just when he would finally have lots of time to spend with his children, they might not have time to spend with him. He was determined to avoid that.

He said, "It reminds me of that song 'Cat's in the Cradle'" (Chapin, Harry, and Sandy Chapin, 1974). At which point Anthony became quite emotional and struggled for composure a few moments.

I can't give all of Harry Chapin's lyrics here. You can easily find them on the Web, which is where I found them. But the story of the song is of a father talking about his son, and how he is too busy to spend time with him, although he wants to. The son, of course, adores his dad and wants to be like him when he grows up. There's a recurring line:

> *I'm gonna be just like you, Dad,*
> *You know, I'm gonna be like you.*

The son grows up and has a family of his own, and a high-powered job, just like Dad. Here's the last verse:

> *I've long since retired, my son's moved away*
> *I called him up just the other day*
> *I said, "I'd like to see you if you don't mind"*
> *He said, "I'd love to, Dad, if I can find the time*
> *You see my new job's a hassle and kids have the flu*
> *But it's sure nice talking to you, Dad*
> *It's been sure nice talking to you"*

Anthony explained that his emotional reaction to thinking about bad retirement outcomes was not that he was like the father in the song. This reaction was far from it, in fact. To some extent, his tears were tears of joy about what he had accomplished with his family. He found it poignant, he said, because the song reminded him of his core value, which was to be a good family man. Being a good husband and father, spending time together as a family, being involved with his children's lives and their work and sports activities at school— all of this was what was most important to him now. And he wanted to make sure that what was described in the song would never apply to him, that those precious family bonds would be there in the future, too, different in many ways, probably, but just as important.

For Anthony, the prospective hindsight exercise had been a reminder and validation of what he values most. You might well have a similar experience.

■

In the next step you will come up against the challenge of predicting your future tastes and preferences.

REFERENCES

Chapin, Harry, and Sandy Chapin. 1974. "Cat's in the Cradle." California: Alfred Music Publishing Co., Inc.
Efstathiou Jr., Jim. 2014. "Oil Supply Surge Brings Calls to Ease U.S. Export Ban," *Bloomberg*, December 16, 2013, accessed February 17, 2014, http://www.bloomberg.com/news/2013-12-17/oil-supply-surge-brings-calls-to-ease-u-s-export-ban.html.

Goldberg, Eleanor. 2014. "Zach Galifianakis to Take Elizabeth 'Mimi' Haist, Homeless Woman He Saved, to 'Hangover III' Premiere." *Huffington Post*, May 20, 2013, accessed February 16, 2014, http://www.huffingtonpost.com/2013/05/20/zach-galifianakis-homeless-friend_n_3306824.html.

Mitchell, Deborah J., J. Edward Russo, and Nancy Pennington. 1989. "Back to the Future: Temporal Perspective in the Explanation of Events." *Journal of Behavioral Decision Making* 2: 25–38.

Myre, Greg. 2014. "The 1973 Arab Oil Embargo: The Old Rules No Longer Apply." NPR, October 16, 2013, accessed February 17, 2014, http://www.npr.org/blogs/parallels/2013/10/15/234771573/the-1973-arab-oil-embargo-the-old-rules-no-longer-apply.

O'Connell, James J. 2005. "Premature Mortality in Homeless Populations: A Review of the Literature." Nashville: National Health Care for the Homeless Council, Inc.

STEP 5

Recognize the Limits of Forecasting

I grew up in Tel Aviv. Although my wife, Lesli, was born in Turkey, she also grew up in Israel. Not surprisingly, Israel is very important to both of us. For some time now we have been fortunate enough to be able to spend several months every summer there, in a condo in Tel Aviv, with our daughter, Maya. We love being there, especially because we are able to spend time with close friends and family.

A dark cloud threatened to disrupt this family tradition, perhaps even end it, during the summer of 2014. I am talking, of course, about the unfortunate conflict between Hamas and Israel in the Gaza Strip. As tensions rose, everyone in Tel Aviv knew that missiles could soon start landing on the city. Lesli and I talked about that possibility and we were pretty sure that the experience would be so awful that we would be on a plane back to the United States at the first attack.

I was on an international conference call—with the team working on this book project, actually—in the safest room in the house when the first air raid siren started to wail. Sure enough, Lesli was stricken with fear, banging on my door. Who wouldn't be? I was. When it all passed, I said to Lesli, "OK, let's get our air tickets and leave." I was certain she would be packing our bags at hyperspeed, ready to scoop up Maya and head for the airport. Instead, she said, "Well, I'm not so sure about that."

When the second siren sounded a few hours later, Lesli's attitude was something like a shrug and "whatever." Mine, too.

When we had thought earlier about the prospects of being under missile attack, we had both predicted that nothing would prevent us from leaving the country immediately. But when that future happened with the first missile, our predictions turned out to be wildly wrong. Yes, there was an initial fright, but it soon passed and we became quite sanguine about the whole thing. Turned out, the sirens and the missiles did not affect us emotionally as much as we thought they would.

This episode was a very personal lesson for me, and one relevant to this step: Predicting one's future feelings, tastes, and preferences is hard—much more difficult than we might imagine.

Behavioral Challenge:
Limits on Predicting Our Preferences

Step 4 described the difficulty we have in predicting outcomes and events because we typically focus too narrowly on one future. The behavioral challenge that my story illustrates, and the topic of Step 5, is the pervasive difficulty we experience in predicting future tastes and preferences. Now, predicting future tastes and preferences is an important part of decision making in life. It touches on matters that range from the relatively trivial to the critical.

You do it, for instance, when you think about what restaurant to visit or decide to go on a weeklong Caribbean cruise in summer, for the first time. Get these judgments of future enjoyment wrong and the worst that can happen is that you have a not very enjoyable restaurant meal or waste a week's vacation time.

Matters become more serious if you fail to predict how well you will enjoy the new job you've just taken or how well you will get along with the new roommate with whom you've just signed a joint lease. And, of course, choosing a spouse is perhaps the ultimate in predicting future tastes and preferences, as you go through life together, with change being inevitable. You marry someone today, you have your set of preferences, she has hers, they match perfectly today. You wind up with a different set, and so does she, now they don't match so well. Getting that decision wrong can have very painful consequences.

Two decades ago, Daniel Kahneman teamed up with Jackie Snell in what became a rather famous demonstration of the poor ability we have of predicting future tastes, even in the simplest of situations (Kahneman and Snell, 1992). The study involved eating plain yogurt, a food that not everyone likes.

Kahneman and Snell gathered about 30 Berkeley students in their lab and gave each of them a spoonful of yogurt and asked them to rate how much they liked or disliked it. The students were then told that they would take home a supply of 6-ounce containers of the same plain yogurt with instructions to finish one container at the end of the day, two hours after their last meal, with no distractions around them, for a week. Before they left the lab they were asked to predict how much they would enjoy eating the container of yogurt on the first day of the study, which was the next day. They were also asked to predict how much they would like or dislike the yogurt on the last day of the study, day eight.

The prediction of taste for day one was, not surprisingly, pretty much as they had experienced it in the lab, which was mild dislike. Most thought that by the eighth day their dislike would have increased, but only mildly so.

Think about it for a moment. We eat all the time, perhaps too often for some of us. We have experience in tasting things and have no trouble saying what we like and don't like. It should therefore have been the easiest thing on the planet for these students to predict their like or dislike of a carton of yogurt on the first day of the study, which was just one day after their first taste, and on day eight, just a week after that first taste. After all, it wasn't as if they were being asked to predict how much they would like the yogurt one or ten years later, react to some entirely new experience or something complicated, like what their preferences are going to be in retirement and how they might change over time.

This is what actually happened in the study. On day one, the rating of the yogurt was extreme dislike. The students hated it. Remember, this was just one day after the students had had their first taste of the yogurt in the lab, so you would expect reasonably accurate predictions. The students had expected to have a mild dislike for the yogurt, just as they had in the lab tasting. They were completely wrong. Perhaps they didn't anticipate their reaction to eating 6 ounces of the yogurt rather than a single spoonful.

By day eight, their initial intense dislike for the yogurt

largely disappeared and the experience came close to what it had been in the lab, but a little more positive. Again, this was contrary to the students' predictions. During the course of the week, the students went from completely hating the yogurt to, if not actually liking it, at least finding it tolerable. So you can see that on this relatively non-challenging test of how well these young people would be able to predict their likes and dislikes over a relatively short time period, they failed quite spectacularly. Who knew?

"[T]he tasks of taste prediction that our subjects performed were surely easier than those which must be confronted in choosing a roommate or a job," wrote Kahneman and Snell. And yet, they note, the answer to the question of what people know about their future tastes is "not much."

In my case, Lesli and I had made the mistake of believing that when the first missile was arcing toward Tel Aviv that summer of 2014, we would be so alarmed that we would immediately want to leave Israel and return to the United States. As you saw, we couldn't have been more wrong.

The behavioral challenge Lesli and I faced, that we all face, is knowing what we will like in the future, what our tastes and preferences will be. It is about knowing what we want and like now and what we will want and like in the future. And, as you now know, we are just not very good at doing that.

Behavioral Solution: Acknowledge Those Limits

A powerful first step toward a solution for this behavioral challenge is awareness. Be aware that the problem exists and that we all fall prey to it. If you remain unaware of this thinking trap, you will not look for a solution, obviously.

The solution is effectively in two parts. The first part is, as I just said, awareness of the problem, which is the goal of this step. The second part, which is to learn from the experience of others, is the goal of the following step.

Thinking About Limits to Forecasting in Retirement Planning

The exercise here is to think about the limits of forecasting, especially about your values and preferences in the distant future. You do it as follows:

> **STEP 5.** Take a moment to think about what you value today. A long time ago, say when you were twenty or thirty years old, would you have predicted these would be your values?

If there is a disconnect between what you value now and what your younger self would have predicted, imagine whether this might apply to your ability to predict what you will value most twenty or thirty years from today. Acknowledge that you are likely to need help in discovering what your tastes and preferences might be in your retirement future. You will find that help in the following chapter, Step 6.

This is how "John," a financial adviser in his forties, responded to the exercise questions:

> When I was twenty I would have predicted that I would value material things more than I do now. I

have come to realize that material things don't bring happiness. That's not what I thought when I was younger.

As you can see, the younger John would have been incorrect in his prediction of what would be important to an older John. We found John's response to be typical.

■

Your journey through the GPS is almost complete. Your next task will be to find some guidance in the experience and perspectives of others, in Step 6.

REFERENCES

Kahneman, Daniel, and Jackie Snell. 1992. "Predicting a Changing Taste: Do people know what they will like?" *Journal of Behavioral Decision Making* 5: 187–200.

STEP 6

Consider the Perspectives of Others

Suppose you are a professional woman in your thirties and you realize that now is the time to meet a potential spouse, someone who will be the father of your child. This is something you haven't made time for in your busy life so far. What do you do? You have no wish to go back to the dating scene you enjoyed as a student, as you feel you've matured beyond that. You have heard about speed dating, so you think you will give it a try.

Speed dating is a bit like a tapas-bar approach to dining. Instead of committing yourself to the usual appetizer-entrée-dessert combination you'd normally follow when eating out, you have a little of this, a little of that, a little of the other. See what food you enjoy most. Only with speed dating it is potential dates you are assessing, not food.

At a typical speed-dating event, women are assigned to tables and are visited by men whose profiles they have read beforehand. Therefore, the women have some idea of who they are going to be conversing with for, say, the next three minutes, or eight minutes, maybe even ten minutes. At which point a signal indicates it's time for the guy to move to another table, and so on until the evening is over. The

speed daters rate each other every time they switch part-
ners, which gives the organizers a way of facilitating fol-
low-up meetings when prospects look good.

So there you are, sitting at a table in a popular downtown
coffee shop. There's a quiet buzz of anticipation in the air.
You are a little nervous, but also excited, because you know
you won't get trapped with a guy you have no interest in.
And, who knows, Mr. Right might be there in the room
with you right now, but you have yet to meet him. You look
down at the piece of paper you've been given with a brief
profile and a photograph of "Harry," whom you are about
to meet. Harry is your age, he's an interesting mix of being
sporty (he plays tennis and is a football fan) and intellectual
(he listens to classical music and reads a lot). He loves to
travel and is something of a foodie.

A bell rings and all of a sudden Harry is standing in front
of you, smiling, extending his hand, and saying, "Sally, isn't
it? May I sit down?" Your heart races a little, and you are
thinking, "Here we go."

The question for you at this moment, Sally, is this: What
kind of information do you think would be more helpful to
you in predicting your experience for the next eight minutes with Harry? Referencing the written profile and photograph on the table in front of you? Or suppose you had
the opportunity instead to hear from some other random
woman, a complete stranger, about her experience of a speed
date with Harry? Which would you opt for: the photograph
and profile or the report from some random woman?

Behavioral Challenge:
More Limits of Forecasting

Here we are facing an extension of the challenge we encountered in the previous chapter, Step 5, which was, surprisingly, how we are limited in our ability to predict our own future tastes and preferences. The famous yogurt experiment reveals that limitation. Rather than predicting on our own, Step 6 focuses on using the help of others to predict. Or, more specifically, what kind of information is most helpful to us when predicting our future feelings and preferences. This was the question for Sally when she was about to meet Harry.

If you are like most people, you would place a lot of weight on what you had read about Harry and on his photograph and on your ability to form an accurate opinion of him based on that information. The notion that a report of a speed-date experience with Harry by a woman you don't know seems to you unlikely to be very helpful. But you would be wrong to think so. Here's why.

We saw in the previous chapter that we are not particularly proficient at predicting our future tastes and preferences or our future likes and dislikes. Indeed, studies demonstrate this lack of proficiency in many areas of life, such as in social, economic, legal, and medical realms. Harvard psychologist Daniel Gilbert, author of *Stumbling on Happiness*, is especially interested in people's likes and dislikes and what can influence them. In a 2009 paper in the journal *Science*, Gilbert and three colleagues point out that people are rather poor at predicting how happy or unhappy they are likely to be, under future good and bad situations (Gilbert et al., 2009). For instance, people tend to overestimate how happy they will be winning a prize (Kermer et al., 2006), initiating a romantic relationship (Gilbert et al., 1998), or taking revenge against those who have harmed them (Carlsmith, Wilson, and Gilbert, 2008). And they overestimate how unhappy they will be after receiving bad test results (Wilson et al., 2004), becoming disabled (Albrecht and Devlieger, 1999), or being denied a promotion (Gilbert et al., 1998).

In that *Science* paper, Gilbert and his colleagues describe a fascinating study on speed dating. Here's the first part of their conclusion:

> People can more accurately predict their affective reactions [likes and dislikes] to a future event when they know how a neighbor in their social network reacted to the event than when they know about the event itself.

You probably find this surprising. You are not alone, because the second part of the conclusion reads as follows:

> People do not believe this.

Gilbert and his colleagues set up a speed-dating service with a small group of Harvard students, most of whom did not know one another. The "get acquainted" sessions were just five minutes. Before each session, the women were provided with either a photograph and profile of the guy they were about to meet, which gave his name, age, height, and his hometown as well as his favorite movie, sport, book, song, food, hangout, and college class, or a report of another woman's speed-date experience with the guy, a number on an "enjoyment scale" from zero to 100, from "not at all" to "very much."

They were then asked to predict how much they expected to enjoy the session on the same enjoyment scale, based on the information they had been given. Before beginning the encounter, the women were provided with the information (profile or report) they had not seen before making their liking prediction, so everyone went into the encounters with the same amount of information.

As I've implied, most people place a lot of confidence in their ability to predict how they will feel about an event in the future when they are given information about that event. We do a mental simulation based on that information and believe we have a good idea about how we will feel when the event occurs. However, that confidence is misplaced, as the speed-dating study demonstrates. Participants in the study were much more accurate in their predictions of enjoyment based on another woman's report than on information in a profile—about twice as accurate, actually.

When you think about it, this result is quite remarkable, because it is not as if every woman would make the same predictions or have the same dating preferences. These predictions are based on the experience of just one random woman whom the speed daters don't know at all. In recognition of this, Gilbert and his colleagues title their paper "The Surprising Power of Neighborly Advice." Surprising, it's true, but significant, and something we should clearly pay attention to.

But here's the telling part, to which I've already alluded: Despite their experience in the study, three-quarters of the women believed that they would have been able to make more accurate predictions had they had profile information and done the mental simulation. Moreover, 84 percent of them said that profile information would enable them to make a more accurate forecast about a future date with a different guy. "When we want to know our emotional futures, it is difficult to believe that a neighbor's experience can provide greater insight than our own best guess," note the study's authors. Apparently, experiencing is not the same as believing.

Gilbert and his colleagues cite the following sage advice for when we are faced with decision-making situations: "Before we set our hearts too much upon anything, let us first examine how happy those are who already have it." Now, you might expect this pearl of wisdom to be the product of some twenty-first-century, Nobel Prize–winning psychologist. In fact, it was coined close to four centuries ago by François de la Rochefoucauld, a seventeenth-century French nobleman famous, to those who know of him, for his book of maxims. You could call it timeless wisdom.

Our robust overconfidence is not confined to forecasting future feelings. For instance, 94 percent of professors judge themselves to be above-average teachers (Cross, 1977). And a staggering 90 percent of us consider ourselves to be above-average drivers (Svenson, 1981).

Behavioral Solution: Learning from Others

When we consider what our future feelings would be in a particular situation, we would benefit from tapping into the experience of someone who has been there. For instance, if you are going to be a new parent, asking existing parents how they experienced the first few months of parenthood will help you prepare in a way that nothing else can. I don't know of any parent who has ever said, "The profound joy I feel looking into my baby's eyes was no surprise for me."

You feel yourself to be different from others, unique in many ways. With that feeling comes a reluctance to believe that you will react to situations in ways similar to other people, that you know better how you will react than they do. That's the behavioral challenge here. You are unique, of course. But you can see now that learning from the experience of others will help you in many different circumstances in life. Listening to others, even strangers, is a powerful thinking tool.

Learning from Others in Retirement Planning

While this step focuses on the power of learning from the experience of others, you need to be wise about whom you consult. You can't know what early parenthood will be like by asking other soon-to-be parents, because they have not experienced that (mostly) happy state. They would probably make the same mistakes that you would make. In the same way, when you want to get insights into how you might feel at various points of retirement, you will benefit most from people who are already in retirement.

Thinking about *why* another person might prioritize one goal as most important and identify another as least important can help you expand your own thinking processes.

STEP 6: So take a few minutes to consider the perspectives of three other people:

1. *Scenario #1:* A sixty-five-year-old woman prioritizes self-improvement over leisure. *Why?*
2. *Scenario #2:* A seventy-five-year-old man prioritizes social engagement over financial independence. *Why?*
3. *Scenario #3:* An eighty-five-year-old woman prioritizes healthcare over travel. *Why?*

Put yourself in the shoes of these three retirees and try to come up with an explanation or narrative as to why these decisions might have been made. I think of this process as an exercise in stretching your mind and actively thinking about what others did when they traveled into that foreign territory.

When you have completed that exercise, feel free to take a look at how retirees in these scenarios thought about their priorities.

RETIREE FOR SCENARIO #1: Margaret, sixty-five, a recently retired university executive, has never been interested in the usual diversions of time off—golfing, lying on the beach, or taking up crosswords. But she's always wanted to finish the Ph.D. in art history she abandoned in her twenties, when she was starting a family. Now the kids are all moved out and she has the time, energy, and passion.

RETIREE FOR SCENARIO #2: Giovanni, seventy-five, a retired plumber, worked hard to make sure he had an adequate retirement fund but he never had time to join his Rotary Club's extended social activities. Now he's got it.

RETIREE FOR SCENARIO #3: Lynn, eighty-five, a retired nurse, traveled a lot with her husband early in retirement; now that he's dead, she has little interest in cruises, tours, and exotic destinations. With a family history of stroke, she wants to get the best cardiovascular expertise she can.

Compare the scenarios you came up with against the stories of Margaret, Giovanni, and Lynn, and reflect on how reading their experiences might have expanded your thinking about your future self and your future preferences. Also note that, not surprisingly, priorities change at different stages along the retirement journey.

■

Your task in the upcoming chapter, Step 7, Reprioritize Goals, is to benefit from the exercises you've been doing in Steps 4 to 6, in reprioritizing your goals for retirement.

REFERENCES

Albrecht, Gary L., and Patrick J. Devlieger. 1999. "The Disability Paradox: High Quality of Life Against All Odds." *Social Science and Medicine* 48, no. 8: 977–988.

Carlsmith, Kevin, Timothy D. Wilson, and Daniel T. Gilbert. 2008. "The Paradoxical Consequences of Revenge." *Journal of Personality and Social Psychology* 95, no. 6: 1316–1324.

Cross, Patricia K. 1977. "Not Can, But Will College Teachers Be Improved?" *New Directions for Higher Education* 17: 1–15.

Gilbert, Daniel T., Elizabeth C. Pinel, Timothy D. Wilson, Stephen J. Blumberg, and Thalia P. Wheatley. 1998. "Immune Neglect: A Source of Durability Bias in Affective Forecasting." *Journal of Personality and Social Psychology* 75: 617–638.

Gilbert, Daniel T., Matthew A. Killingsworth, Rebecca N. Eyre, and Timothy D. Wilson. 2009. "The Surprising Power of Neighborly Advice." *Science* 323: 1617–1619.

Kermer, Deborah A., Erin Driver-Linn, Timothy D. Wilson, and Daniel T. Gilbert. 2006. "Loss Aversion Is an Affective Forecasting Error." *Psychological Science* 17: pp. 649–653.

Svenson, Ola. 1981. "Are We All Less Risky and More Skillful Than Our Fellow Drivers?" *Acta Psychologica* 47: 143–148.

Wilson, Timothy D., Thalia P. Wheatley, Jaime L. Kurtz, Elizabeth W. Dunn, and Daniel T. Gilbert. 2004. "When to Fire: Anticipatory Versus Postevent Reconstrual of Uncontrollable Events." *Personality and Social Psychology Bulletin* 30, no. 3: 340–351.

STEP 7

Reprioritize Goals

Suppose you are meeting for the first time with your new financial adviser, Mary. At the top of the agenda is how to structure your portfolio. The question of what proportion of your portfolio you should allocate to stocks is front and center. This is an important decision, one that you are aware should be weighed with great care.

In the middle of the discussion your cell phone rings and you see that the call is from your daughter. You always interrupt what you are doing when she calls in case it is something urgent. "Daddy," she says, obviously excited, "you aren't going to believe this. I got 91 points on my math exam today!" You say, "Wow! Really?" Very proud of her achievement, she repeats it. "Yes, really, 91 points." You are proud, too, of course, and you say, "91 points, that's a very high score." "Yes it is, Daddy," she says, "91 points was the highest in class." You tell her that you will celebrate together this evening but that right now you must get back to talking with your financial adviser.

You turn back to Mary, who immediately congratulates you and says, "Wow, 91 points. That's impressive." You smile broadly, and nod enthusiastically. Proud Dad. Now it is back to business.

Mary lays out three portfolio options. The first has 60 percent in stocks, the second has 72 percent, and the third has 84 percent. You find yourself strongly drawn to the last of the three, the one with 84 percent in stocks. Why? Because, you tell yourself, it fits your investment objectives and the current investment climate.

Question: Could there be another factor, perhaps a totally irrelevant factor, that drove your decision to invest 84 percent in stocks rather than either of the lower options?

Behavioral Challenge: Anchoring on Status Quo

Working stealthily and out of your consciousness is the figure "91," acting like a magnet on your decision making, leading you to opt for the highest of the portfolio options. A number that is lurking in your mind at that point, and one that has absolutely nothing to do with the merits of the decision you are about to make, nevertheless strongly influences your decision.

If you find this story verges on the absurd, because of its lack of rationality, you would be in good company. Traditional theories in economics tell us that people make decisions rationally and are influenced only by what is relevant to the decision. Irrelevant information should have no influence whatsoever, and yet, as you saw in the story I told, your daughter's stellar performance on the math test helped shape your investment strategy for years to come.

Now, I have to admit, the story is just that, a story, a

hypothetical case I tell my students. But it is soundly based on research that we have a tendency to be distracted by factors that have nothing to do with the matter at hand, leading us to less-than-rational decisions or judgments. We've seen examples of such thinking traps in earlier chapters. In this case the thinking trap, or behavioral challenge, is known as anchoring (or, more correctly, anchoring and adjustment) (Tversky and Kahneman, 1974).

Here's one of the scores of examples of the phenomenon called anchoring in psychology literature, one that, I have to say, is a little unsettling.

You would expect, or at least hope, that a court of law is one place where relevant evidence, and only relevant evidence, influences decisions, in this case judicial decisions by judges. The study involved German judges with an average of fifteen years of experience in trying criminal cases. They were asked to read the case of a woman convicted of shoplifting. Before recommending a sentence, the judges were asked to roll a pair of dice, which, without their knowledge, were loaded, so that every roll wound up as a 3 or a 9. Immediately after the dice were rolled, the judges were asked whether the sentence they would recommend would be more or less, in months, than the number shown on the dice. The judges were then asked to be specific about their sentence for the shoplifter.

It's hard to believe, but the results of the study show that the sentences the judges handed down were heavily influenced by the tally of the dice they had rolled. On average, those who had rolled a 9 said they would sentence the woman to eight months while those who rolled a 3 gave a much more lenient judgment, five months on average (Englich, Mussweiler, and Strack, 2006). So here you have experienced professionals doing what they do every day, which is hand out judicial decisions, and yet their judgment is heavily influenced by a totally irrelevant piece of information, the roll of a pair of dice. Einstein famously said that God does not play dice with the universe, yet here in this small corner of the universe dice exert undue influence.

This is a strong anchoring effect in a situation where there is a reasonable expectation that outside factors, especially irrelevant outside factors, would have no influence. As I said, it is just one of many such demonstrations, each of which is just as jaw-dropping in their defiance of expectations (Kahneman, 2011).

The phenomenon of anchoring is a cogent reminder of the propensity of fast thinking to lead us astray. It has been described as "arguably one of the most important truths about human judgment" (Simmons, LeBoeuf, and Nelson, 2010). Indeed, studies have shown that even when participants are told that an anchor (an irrelevant number) might sway their answer to a question (how many physicians are in the local phone book, for example), they aren't able to fully escape its influence (Wilson et al., 1996; Simmons, LeBoeuf, and Nelson, 2010).

The behavioral challenge, then, is that when we are making a decision we can be unduly influenced by information that is in front of us, coursing subtly through our mind. And it's surprising that, first, we are completely unaware of that fact and, second, that we are vulnerable to this powerful anchoring effect whether or not the information is relevant to the decision at hand.

Behavioral Solution:
Whiteboard Exercise

Studies that find that participants are still influenced to some degree by anchors, even when they are alerted to that danger, imply that there is no simple, fully effective behavioral solution. There is nothing like a master list to overcome thinking blind spots, for example. You can, however, employ what we call the Whiteboard Exercise to help minimize the influence of anchors. The exercise is just as it sounds: When you are faced with a decision, try to start with a clean slate—start fresh.

Here's one scenario: You structured your retirement portfolio maybe twenty, thirty, years ago. You have probably made minor adjustments every year but you have never rethought the overall strategy. You are now in retirement and are no longer earning money. Instead, you are only spending money. So you have a new problem, which is how to generate a paycheck without actually working anymore. And maybe you are using a solution that is decades old. To get you thinking into the "now" you need to think fresh, and that is difficult unless you push away everything from the past.

Here's a smart way for Mary, our financial adviser, to be in a position to help you start fresh. Mary can simply ignore your current portfolio, not even look at it. She can ask for the total value of your portfolio (but not its structure) and discuss with you your short- and longer-term goals, your level of risk tolerance, and so on. She can then come up with options that suit you today without being anchored on your decisions from the past. That is the Whiteboard Exercise. It is an attempt to avoid being influenced by what is out there on the decision table that reflects the past, so to speak. It can also be quite effective in addressing your goals for retirement.

The Whiteboard Exercise in Retirement Planning

At the end of the first part of this book, you had generated a master list of goals and, painful though the process was, you allocated them to three buckets—most-important, moderately important, and least-important goals—using the goal tiles and prioritization board you either accessed via the electronic version of the tool or downloaded from http://www .retirementgoalplanningsystem.com. This current chapter, Step 7, offers you the opportunity to reprioritize them as a result of the exercises you undertook in Steps 4, 5, and 6.

You could stay with the prioritized list you produced in Step 3 if you so choose, because, after all, you would be in a more thought-out position with regard to your plans for retirement than when you started this book. But the intent of the exercises in Steps 4, 5, and 6 was to get you to go deeper, bringing other thoughts and information to mind to improve the overall retirement planning process. Now is the time to put that extra work into action, to reprioritize, again using your prioritization board.

But I urge you, in the face of the anchoring challenge, to go through the Whiteboard Exercise. Try to imagine, as hard as you can, that your first prioritized list does not exist and that you are prioritizing for the first time. It is an opportunity to rethink, to be open to something new.

Here is what you do:

STEP 7: Clear the prioritization board, paper or electronic, you used earlier. Now go through the goal-prioritization exercise described in Step 3, for a second time. You can put aside any goals that you feel no longer apply, or add ones that do.

Once you have completed this step, congratulations! You have arrived at a newly prioritized list of goals for your retirement, the product of going deeper this time. It is possible, as I said earlier, that your newly constructed list will be identical to the one you produced at the end of Step 3, in which case, wonderful! You probably have a good list. More than likely, however, the Whiteboard Exercise, and subsequent reprioritization, will generate something different from earlier, perhaps dramatically so.

REFERENCES

Englich, Birte, Thomas Mussweiler, and Fritz Strack. 2006. "Playing Dice with Criminal Sentences: The Influence of Irrelevant Anchors on Experts' Judicial Decision Making." *Personality and Social Psychology Bulletin* 32: 188–200.

Kahneman, Daniel. 2011. Chapter on "Anchors" in *Thinking, Fast and Slow*. New York: Farrar, Straus and Giroux.

Simmons, Joseph P., Robyn A. LeBoeuf, and Lief D. Nelson. 2010. "The Effect of Accuracy Motivation on Anchoring and Adjustment: Do People Adjust from

Provided Anchors?" *Journal of Personality and Social Psychology* 99, no. 6: 917–932.

Tversky, Amos, and Daniel Kahneman. 1974. "Judgment Under Uncertainty: Heuristics and Biases." *Science* 185: 1124–1131.

Wilson, Timothy D., Christopher E. Houston, Nancy Brekke, and Kathryn M. Etling. 1996. "A New Look at Anchoring Effects: Basic Anchoring and Its Antecedents." *Journal of Experimental Psychology* 125, no. 4: 387–402.

Steps 4–7 in Action

You have just worked through a series of thinking tools—Steps 4 to 7—specially designed to help you go even deeper in discovering your goals for your future and what is going to be most important to you in your retirement years. Francesca and Phillip also went through this process of thinking. Here is an opportunity to witness how they experienced the process.

You will recall that both Francesca and Phillip finished up with prioritized lists of goals that had evolved in unexpected ways during Steps 1 to 3. For Francesca, one of her three most important goals, financial independence, had not even been on her initial list of goals. And ending life with dignity, which had also been absent from her initial list, she now considered a moderately important goal. In Phillip's case, two of his moderately important goals—family bequest and ending life with dignity—weren't on his initial list of self-identified goals. The thinking tools in Steps 1 to 3 had broadened and deepened Francesca and Phillip's thinking, giving them the help they obviously needed. That all of us need. You probably experienced that, too.

Now let's see the impact of Steps 4 to 7 on further deepening their thinking, beginning with Francesca.

Francesca's Journey

The first of these steps, Step 4, Think Beyond One Future, asks us to first imagine a really good retirement outcome (Step 4A) and, second, a really bad retirement outcome (Step 4B). These are Francesca's responses:

STEP 4A: "A good outcome for me would be that I am doing something that I love, which allows me to give back, is paying some of the bills, and gives me a real sense of fulfillment. I have some ideas about what this might be, but I am still fairly vague as yet. I am healthy and I spend a lot of time outdoors, hiking— and doing yoga. Ideally, I am living in a small but charming place in Northern California. I would be seeing old friends a lot, have many new friends, and would be able to see my family whenever I wanted to. I don't need a lot."

STEP 4B: "In a really bad retirement outcome I would be very alone, struggling financially, and unable to see family very often. I would be living in a small apartment, probably in an urban environment. Although I love the city, I would be crushed to have to live in an apartment where what I see when I open my door is a corridor leading to an elevator instead of a beautiful yard. My health wouldn't be great; I wouldn't be able to walk and hike and do yoga. And I wouldn't have been giving back, as I'd hoped. Looking back, I would see that my life had all been downhill from where I am now, that where I am now was the high point. That would be really bad."

Now that you've seen Francesca's imagined "good" and "bad" retirement outcomes, you can try a thought experiment and guess how she might want to change her goals as a result of this exercise. What goal(s) might become more important? Hint: Look at the very powerful emotional word right at the beginning of Step 4B, that is, being "alone." We'll find out the answer in Step 7 when Francesca will reprioritize her goals after going through additional thinking exercises.

Step 5 of GPS asks you to think about how your younger self would have predicted how your future values would unfold. Then you can compare that prediction with what actually transpired in your life. The following is Francesca's response for Step 5:

"At the top of the list of what I value now is the idea of giving back, of using the skills and knowledge I've acquired over the years to help others in my community and at large. There's a sense of urgency about this. I really do want to contribute something significant before I shuffle off this mortal coil and one can never know when that will happen. Although the idea of giving back has always been on my mind, it wouldn't have been at the top of the list of what I thought was important in life. So this is a surprise for me. My recent confrontation with my own mortality has made me want to do more to help others and to do it now instead of deferring it until later."

You can see, then, that the younger Francesca would have been decidedly wrong in her predictions of her future values, tastes, and preferences. Your younger self was probably no fortune-teller either, just like Francesca's.

Step 6 of the GPS exercise involves looking at the top retirement goals of three individuals, one sixty-five years old, the second seventy-five, and the third eighty-five. Each has different goals, of course. The person doing the exercise, Francesca in this case, then describes how each retiree might have come to their decision, and then reflects on her own thinking at this stage in the whole process.

Francesca was drawn to the decisions of the 65-year-old retiree, Margaret, who identified self-improvement as her most important goal, with travel and leisure as her least important one. "I can completely see how this person might have had some area of interest they had wanted to pursue earlier in their life but for one reason or another, they had put it on the back burner," says Francesca. "Maybe studying art history, something like that. Anyway, now that she is entering retirement she can resurrect that long-quiescent interest and put it on the front burner, at last." Francesca speculated that Margaret might have had to travel a lot for her work, so travel no longer appeals to her. In any case, Margaret wants to fully concentrate on her drive for self-improvement.

Although Francesca resonated most strongly with Margaret, she could readily see why 75-year-old Giovanni puts social engagement as a top priority. "Maybe Giovanni realizes that with family no longer close by he has to actively seek other ways of interacting socially," says Francesca. "I can completely see that." Francesca can also see why Lynn, 85, puts her healthcare as a high priority given her age and family history of stroke and she can also relate to Margaret's priorities given her own recent health scare.

Despite their different ages and top priorities, Margaret, Giovanni, and Lynn each influenced Francesca's thinking in different ways. "Margaret's focus on self-improvement made me think a lot about that for me," says Francesca, "given where I am in my life right now. But it did more than that. It made me see how interconnected these goals can be.

For instance, I expect that giving back, one of my top goals in Step 3, will lead me into activities that I would categorize as self-improvement. In turn, being involved with others when I'm doing volunteer work will also present opportunities for social engagement."

Francesca commented that the experience of thinking about these other three lives and their particular perspectives didn't completely change her thinking, but it definitely made her think more deeply about her goals and how she prioritizes them.

The last step in the GPS journey for Francesca, Step 7, was to reprioritize her goals. The following is her new list:

- Most important: financial independence, giving back, healthcare
- Moderately important: lifestyle, housing, self-improvement, social engagement
- Least important: travel and leisure, ending life with dignity, second career

As you can see, Francesca didn't change a lot. Except for one important thing. "There is a big part of me that likes being alone," she says. "But when I want to be with people, I really want to be with people. I realized that social engagement was something I was likely to miss when I stopped working and particularly as I grow older." As a result of this thinking, Francesca moved social engagement up on her list of priorities from being among the "least important" to being one of her "moderately important" goals. Remember, being alone was the first thing that came to mind when Francesca was imagining a bad retirement outcome, so going through that process prompted that change in priorities.

Francesca's decision to upgrade social engagement on

her reprioritized list fits a pattern we have seen over and over as different people have worked through the GPS exercise. It is all too easy to take for granted the fact that in our work environments we are surrounded by people, and that social engagement is an integral part of our daily lives. It is only when we think deeply, guided by the GPS exercise, that we recognize how important certain things are to us, and that we would miss it.

Phillip's Journey

Now let's examine Phillip's journey through Steps 4 to 7. Here are his responses to describing a really good retirement (Step 4A) and a really bad one (Step 4B).

> STEP 4A: "A good retirement would be that both of us live long, healthy lives, which would allow us to travel as well as live in multiple places. We both love to think about interesting issues, so a good retirement would allow us to continue to do that. I have a great love for California, but my wife is from New England so I don't think we will ever leave here. I can imagine four months in New England, four months in California, four months on the road, to exotic places like Israel. I have never been to Asia and would love to visit."

> STEP 4B: "The worst case would be losing Joanna early. I don't know what I would do without her. Early onset of mental diminishment would be devastating to me, because being able to think about complex issues defines who I am; and I would hate to be a burden on Joanna. I have seen this happen in my family, so I know how hard it can be for those affected and for their caregivers."

Earlier in the book I mentioned the issue of risks when facing retirement, specifically the risk of early death. You can see from Francesca's and Phillip's worst-case scenarios that other risks can disrupt even the most thoughtfully planned retirement. Some are quite obvious and practical, such as a downturn in the stock market eroding retirement savings. Others are more insidious, such as cognitive impairment. According to the Alzheimer's Association, nearly one in three seniors dies with Alzheimer's or some other dementia (Alzheimer's Association, 2013). Phillip was sensitive to this risk because of family history and the value he places on being able to think clearly.

This is how Phillip's younger self would have predicted his future to unfold, according to Step 5:

"When I was young I imagined my future self scouring the archives of antiquity in libraries, museums, and perhaps archaeological sites in the Old World, with the goal of writing history books that, while not quite up to the stature of the works of my hero, Edward Gibbon, of course, would nevertheless be an important contribution to the annals of historical thought and insight. And now look where I am, an academic economist studying the efficiency of markets, which is not only important in the real world, but work I also love. Well, I suppose there is a historical aspect to this, Adam Smith and all that. But still, not what I would ever have predicted!"

Francesca's and Phillip's stories for Step 5 demonstrate clearly, I think you will agree, that predicting future tastes and preferences is difficult. Some people might see their future selves clearly at a young age, strive for that goal and eventually arrive where they expected to be. But for most of us the task proves elusive. This is a useful lesson, given that you are now trying to predict your tastes and preferences in an older you. You probably need help.

Like Francesca, in Step 6 of the GPS exercise Phillip was asked to think about why three retirees, Margaret, Giovanni, and Lynn, aged sixty-five, seventy-five, and eighty-five, might have selected the most- and least-important goals that they had. "I found the exercise helpful for a couple of reasons," Phillip said. "First, it stirred up thoughts that had been pretty much below the surface, such as self-improvement, and what that might look like. And it gave me a better perspective of retirement as a whole, especially changing needs as we get older."

Here is Phillip's reprioritized list of goals, Step 7:

♦ Most important: financial independence, travel, self-improvement
♦ Moderately important: family bequest
♦ Least important: healthcare, ending life with dignity

For comparison, here is Phillip's initial list of priorities, produced through the step 3 process:

♦ Most important: financial independence, travel
♦ Moderately important: family bequest, ending life with dignity
♦ Least important: healthcare

You can see that Phillip didn't change many items in his newly prioritized list, but there was one huge difference. Namely, he realized that now, or very soon, was the time to focus on what he characterized as "self-improvement," which had not appeared at all in Steps 1–3. How did that happen? Well, when Phillip did Step 6, he immediately resonated with Margaret's desire to reconnect with a long-unfulfilled passion, which was to finish her Ph.D. This recognition in another individual prompted Phillip to seriously consider leaving the post he had held for 30-plus years so that he could spend more time on topics that had recently come to fascinate him a lot, including reading more history books and traveling to historic sites. "One of my happiest memories of recent years is of going to Israel and visiting Caesarea, about half an hour south of Haifa, Israel," he says. "It was the former Roman capital of Palestine. I tell people there, 'You can't go anywhere in your country without stepping on history.'"

Notice that this big change in Phillip's life—self-improvement through leaving behind his successful career and following a new direction—was completely absent in his initial list of goals, until he embarked on Step 7. It then not only became a part of his list but also leaped to being one of the most important goals. This is testimony to the power of the GPS process.

Next Steps for Francesca and Phillip

The experience of going through the GPS exercise propelled Francesca and Phillip into making changes in their lives that surprised not only themselves but also others around them. You will see these changes unfold in this section. Here I label the action steps they took and frame them as a general lesson for all pre-retirees to consider, if these steps fit their circumstances. It is important to bear in mind that each of us has goals, values, and preferences that are our own, and not others'.

I will start with Francesca. Recall that her three top goals were financial independence, giving back, and healthcare.

The following are her top three action items, prompted by the outcomes of the GPS exercise.

1. Tailored Retirement

When Francesca did the GPS exercise she had already begun to think about her life, where she was at just that moment, what she might do in the future. But it wasn't what you would call sitting down and thinking hard, with the intention of making plans for changes in her future. It was more like idly turning over vague possibilities, quietly ruminating at the back of her mind, if you will. What the GPS exercise did was to bring into sharp focus things she was barely aware of, things she now recognized as being important to her, and demanded action. Now!

Recall that Francesca was approaching fifty when she did the exercise, an age most people would regard as mid-career. When she announced at her office that she was going to retire, her colleagues were understandably shocked. Francesca was more than a little shocked herself, truth be told. "I felt I had no option," she says. "The exercise made me see very clearly that 'giving back' was extremely important to me, that it could no longer be something I might get to, some day. I had to act on that realization, *now*."

Francesca's urgency to change her life as a consequence of what she learned about herself through the exercise was also honed by her recent health scare, an event that reminded her of risks in life that can come out of nowhere and disrupt whatever plans we might have. The paycheck and health benefits she enjoyed at her job were nice to have, Francesca acknowledged. But she now recognized that they were, as she put it, "not enough."

But, how would she sustain herself while she fulfilled her need to give back? A friend, knowing of Francesca's passion for yoga, told her he had heard something about yoga for executive women in New York City. It sparked a brilliant idea in her. "I could do what I love, yoga, and earn some money part-time as a yoga teacher," she said, "not in Manhattan, but maybe I could start something in a city in Northern California, San Francisco, perhaps." This idea sparked another one. "I could go to India and learn to become a yoga teacher from a master. I've always wanted to do that. This could be part of my giving back, if I were to give classes for cancer patients and others with life-threatening diseases. So the financial aspect would be covered by teaching yoga to executives and giving back by helping others cope with illness. In any case, being a part-time yoga teacher would ensure that I am frequently in the company of like-minded people. That would be very important to me, to maintain that kind of active social engagement."

So, you can see that the GPS exercise set in motion a series of interconnected ideas that transformed Francesca's life. I haven't seen her so happy in the many years I've known her.

GENERAL LESSON:

Everyone is different and has unique needs and desires. Half-retirement at a very early age will enable Francesca to fulfill her desire to give back and at the same time develop further an activity she loves, yoga. Other people find their careers completely rewarding and work way past the traditional retirement age of sixty-five. Phillip, for example, was nearing seventy when he did the GPS exercise and still in a job he'd been doing for thirty-plus years, and loving it. And my dad, who is seventy-eight, is still working one day a week as a consultant.

Tailored Retirement is all about doing what best fits *your* needs.

2. Claim More Tomorrow

Financial independence is important to Francesca (although, surprisingly, she missed it in Step 1 when she self-generated her list of goals). Being a part-time yoga teacher will help supplement savings in the short term. But Francesca is concerned about running out of money, if she were to live very long. In the longevity lottery, no one knows the outcome, but the story of Jeanne Calment, a Frenchwoman, is instructive.

In 1965, when Madame Calment was ninety, André-François Raffray, a lawyer, offered to pay her the equivalent of $500 a month until she died, a financial instrument called a "reverse mortgage." He would then own her grand apartment in the town of Arles, of Vincent van Gogh fame. Raffray thought he had a terrific deal. After all, Madame Calment was already past the average life expectancy and would surely die before too long. The apartment would then be his, perhaps for just a few thousand dollars.

Thirty-two years later, in April 1997, Madame Calment died at age 122 years, having outlived Raffray by two years (Whitney, 1997). At the time of his death, Raffray had paid the supercentenarian more than $184,000 for an apartment worth only half that amount, and one he never got to live in. At age 113, Madame Calment earned a place in the Guinness Book of World Records as the oldest living person, so her case is extreme. But you just never know. Being concerned about running out of money is a legitimate issue for any retiree.

In Francesca's case, her intuition was to start claiming a Social Security check as soon as she became eligible, at age sixty-two, so as to guarantee a lifetime stream of income. Being only fifty when she "retired," Francesca would have to wait a dozen years before she tapped into that financial pot. This enforced wait wound up being a blessing, as the common rule of thumb of "retire and claim" was not available to her. She therefore had to think deeper about her options and strategy. Francesca decided to live off her savings and her earnings as a part-time yoga teacher during her fifties, draw on her 401(k) accounts in her sixties, and defer claiming Social Security benefits until she hit seventy.

One reason to Claim More Tomorrow, as I call this strategy, is that deferring Social Security benefits is a really good investment. For instance, an individual whose monthly Social Security benefit would be $1,000 at age sixty-two could increase it to $1,760 by waiting to claim it until age seventy. More generally, if an individual uses savings anywhere between the ages of sixty-two and seventy to finance the delay of claiming Social Security benefits, the estimated rate of return above inflation ranges between 5.4 and 7.7 percent each year (Sass, 2012). The other reason that deferring Social Security is a great investment is that deferring Social Security benefits provides certain guarantees that are hard (or at least expensive) to purchase in the marketplace. For instance, Social Security benefits are indexed to increases in cost of living (at least partially), so if Francesca ended up living very long and the cost of living spiked, she would still receive a monthly paycheck that included cost of living adjustments, no matter how long she lived. "Buying" that type of guarantee from the Social Security administration is much cheaper than trying to get it in the marketplace, through annuities for instance.

An important aspect of your claiming strategy for Social Security benefits is how they impact your spouse. What benefits will your spouse continue to receive if you were to die first, for instance? Other considerations include whose benefits to draw on first, among other things. For an insightful and crystal-clear analysis of these issues, read "Efficient Retirement Design," a Stanford Institute for Economic Policy briefing by John B. Shoven and Sita N. Slavov (Shoven and Slavov, 2013).

GENERAL LESSON:

Just because you have retired, or just because you can start claiming Social Security benefits at 62, does not mean it is a financially sound decision. Claim More Tomorrow should be considered as an option.

3. Proactive Health Management

Francesca is concerned about being healthy. Her health scare made her super-sensitive to that. And also to being able to pay to stay healthy. Her strategy to stay healthy is to focus on her lifestyle. She made the active commitment to spend a lot of time outdoors, hiking and enjoying nature as well as committing to a serious personal yoga practice (beyond being a yoga teacher). All of these activities help maintain physical (and mental) health. In addition, she committed to keeping to a sensible diet. In other words, she wasn't going to try to lock herself into what are usually unsustainably strict dietary regimens. Instead she would adhere to what might be called the Julia Child diet, that is, consume what you enjoy, but in moderation. Again, this is also good for physical and mental health. I think of this approach as Proactive Health Management.

In order to help pay for future medical expenses, Francesca decided to invest a portion of her portfolio in the healthcare sector. That way, if medical expenses keep going up, her portfolio will go up too, providing her with extra dollars to pay for the increasing cost of medical expenses. From age sixty-five, the average retiree pays $260,000 in out-of-pocket medical expenses (Webb and Zhivan, 2010), so being able to cover at least some of the extra costs is good for your pocket and your mental health.

GENERAL LESSON:

Francesca's strategy to managing her health as well as her healthcare costs is a constructive approach. After all, it is better to take steps to keep yourself healthy rather than just make sure you have sufficient funds to pay medical bills when you eventually get sick. The best way to manage healthcare costs is to be proactive and manage your health! In other words, Proactive Health Management.

■

So you see that the process of coming to a reprioritized set of retirement goals propelled Francesca into deciding to "retire" at the young age of fifty, which, as I said earlier, was a shock to her colleagues and to a significant degree to Francesca herself. It was to be a "half-retirement," as we saw, which allowed Francesca to fulfill two dreams at once:

first, going to an exotic place to train to become a yoga teacher and, second, to spend more time in her personal yoga practice.

At the same time, the income as a yoga teacher will help sustain Francesca financially so that she can fulfill her other recently realized dream—devoting time to "giving back," something that had been close to her heart for many years but had lain dormant until now. Her decision to delay claiming Social Security fits very well into a longer-term strategy for financial independence at successive phases of her life. And devoting so much time to doing yoga, as well as other physical activities, becomes an integral part of Francesca's Proactive Health Management strategy.

Notice how the initial big surprise to retire at fifty opened up the opportunity for a cascade of interrelated decisions that set Francesca on a firm footing toward her ultimate goal, a happy and fulfilling life after her time in the Big Corporate World.

■

I now turn to Phillip, whose position in his career and life, and his tastes and preferences, you will remember, are generally quite different from Francesca's, although they do share financial independence as a top priority.

Here is a quick reminder of his most important goals from Step 7: financial independence, travel, self-improvement.

I frame Phillip's top action items in general terms, as follows.

1. Spend More Today

Phillip loves to travel but having had parents who went through the Great Depression and hearing stories from them about those grinding years make it difficult for Phillip to justify spending much on travel for himself, just for pleasure. Recall that most of Phillip's travel was primarily work-related, with perhaps a couple of days "to play" tagged on to each trip.

While many Americans spend too much, Phillip might be one of those who are spending too little. Yes, those people do exist. For instance, one study found that, on average, households aged sixty to sixty-nine with personal retirement accounts (401(k)'s, IRA's, and so on) withdraw only about two percent of their account balances each year, which was considerably less than the rate of return on account balances during the time of the study. Even at older ages—after the required minimum distribution age of seventy and a half—the percentage of balances withdrawn remains at about five percent (Poterba, Venti, and Wise, 2011). This evidence, of course, is just suggestive of not spending enough, as people might want to leave money to their kids or play it safe in case they live very long and get hit with unexpected medical bills.

Another study found that while 40 percent of respondents who inherited money and believed they would receive between $10,000 and $50,000 in inheritance ended up inheriting more than they expected, another 40 percent had their expectations met, and only 20 percent wound up being disappointed as they inherited less than expected (Brown, Coile, and Weisbenner, 2010). I suspect that many benefactors could have spent more on themselves than they actually did, before they died. Again, this evidence is suggestive of underspending by retirees.

Phillip most definitely has been an under-spender most of his life. The GPS exercise broadened his horizons and helped him see the potential pleasure of spending in his later years. In what in his "previous life" he would have thought of as a wild and unjustifiable extravagance, he has now committed to flying international business class with his wife to exotic locations and staying in five-star hotels once a year. He estimates that with judicious booking well in advance, the cost would be around $25,000 a year, which he can definitely afford. "We would get a lot of pleasure from that," says Phillip. Notice that Phillip elected to splurge, not on material objects, such as a new luxury car; but rather on experiences that would bring a lot of happiness at the time, and in their memories. This is a wise decision, as you will see below.

The GPS exercise had led Phillip to follow a strategy of what I call Spend More Today.

GENERAL LESSON:

The advertising industry puts a lot of effort into trying to convince us we will be happy if we buy more material things—cars, watches, expensive suits, and so on. By contrast, the slogan of the Center for a New American Dream says, "More fun, less stuff." Which is correct?

Studies on real-life experiences, and in the laboratory, strongly support the latter. "Our research suggests that individuals will live happier lives if they invest in experiences more than material possessions," write psychologists Leaf van Boven and Thomas Gilovich, based on a series of their own studies, and reflecting on others. "By the same token, communities will have happier citizens if they make available an abundance of experiences to be acquired" (Van Boven and Gilovich, 2003). Think of that really great bottle of wine you have stored carefully away. What good is it if you can't drink it with close family and friends and share that wonderful *experience*?

2. The Personal Pension Plan

Phillip cares about financial independence. He'd like a nice monthly paycheck no matter how long he and his wife live. He is especially concerned about his wife's being secure, should he die before she does, which, given their age differences and the different longevity of men and women, is likely. Phillip's approach to thinking about retirement exemplifies the importance of thinking not just of oneself but also of one's spouse. Although it is a topic many shy away from actively thinking about, Phillip wants to make sure that Joanna has all her material needs met, should she one day be alone.

Now that he is approaching seventy, Phillip is expecting a modest check from Social Security, but that check is not enough to pay for all of his basic expenses. Seeing some of his colleagues at other universities getting large monthly checks in the form of traditional pension payments, Phillip decided to purchase what we'll call a "Personal Pension Plan." These products are often called "annuities"* and in

---

* Full disclosure: Allianz Life Insurance of North America (Allianz), a sister company of Allianz Global Investors, is a leading provider of retirement solutions, including fixed and variable annuities and life insurance for individuals. Benartzi is Chief Behavioral Economist of the Allianz Global Investors Center for Behavioral Finance.

their simplest form they work like this: You give an insurance company a lump sum (say $100,000) and in return you receive a monthly paycheck for as long as you live (say $500 every month). Some annuities can be customized, such as to provide for income as long as you live or to provide your spouse with a percentage of income if he/she outlives you. This is something Phillip would certainly do.

Personal Pension Plans are not as popular as you might think they'd be, given the benefits they provide, because some people see them as risky. If you give that big check to the insurer and then die tomorrow, you've lost a lot of money and the prospect of that is emotionally painful. Phillip, however, does not think of his Personal Pension Plan as an investment. Rather, he thinks of it as a consumption plan, the guarantee of a monthly check for life, an insurance of future security, and through these lenses the strategy seems attractive. The willingness to buy annuities has been shown to depend on how they are framed: Annuities framed as consumption plans are much more attractive than when they are framed as investment plans (Brown, et al., 2008; Benartzi, Previtaro, and Thaler, 2011).

Phillip then noticed that by purchasing a Personal Pension Plan that guarantees his basic expenses for life, he can actually "gift now" to his kids. His basic expenses are already covered, so he can use additional funds he has saved to help his kids while they are still young with down payments on their houses and other expenses.

GENERAL LESSON:

Think of goals, plural, not just one individual goal at a time. By purchasing a Personal Pension Plan, Phillip secured financial independence as well as being able to bequest early. Another example of one action addressing multiple goals might involve housing. By moving to community housing, one can downsize and save money as well as boost social engagement.

3. Time as an Asset

Phillip set self-improvement as one of his top priorities. A big part of this will be to read a whole lot more history than he's had time for these past three decades. For instance, on a recent cross-country road trip to California he took with him Prit Buttar's recently published *Collision of Empires*. Phillip explained to me that the book is an account of the little-known but tumultuous events involving the clash of empires on the Eastern Front, between Imperial Germany, Hapsburg Austria-Hungary, and Tsarist Russia, in 1914. (Gives you an idea of Phillip's appetite for historical detail.) But Phillip also plans to be hands-on in delving back into his first love, history, by finding a way to do a research project on some aspect of the Roman Empire and perhaps write a book, which would bring him full circle to that boy in junior high, reading Gibbon's *Decline and Fall of the Roman Empire*, all those years ago. Phillip now can't wait to get to it.

GENERAL LESSON:

Retirement is about our portfolio of resources, which include both financial assets and other assets such as time. Deciding how we spend our retirement is critical to our well-being. Tons of literature on happiness and well-being exist, and one of the potential "tricks" to boost one's well-being is to rethink how we spend time. For example, studies show that, not surprisingly, most of us like eating or engaging in leisure activities more than we like commuting or doing household chores (Kahneman et al., 2006). So, if you, too, enjoy leisure activities much more than household chores, maybe you should hire someone to deal with those chores and spend your time enjoying a nice evening walk with your spouse. Of course, the prescription here needs to be tailored to your individual likes and dislikes, but the general lesson still applies—how you spend your time might be one of the easiest tricks to boost well-being.

■

You have seen that Phillip's experience of reprioritizing his goals (Step 7) prompted him to consider whether he now might to want to change his career path, just as it did for Francesca. Unlike Francesca, who took a dramatic change of direction many years before typical retirement age, Phillip had been completely fulfilled pursuing the career he embarked upon early in his working life. He continued way past typical retirement age. However, the exercise did rekindle interest in his first love, history, and he decided at last to return to it, and actively so. That was an important change in his life.

At the same time, Phillip decided to break a long-standing pattern and splurge on luxurious travel once a year, an experience he was certain he and Joanna would enjoy enormously. He also made sure that he and Joanna were financially secure enough to do this, to cover basic living expenses, with sufficient money available to give to his children early when they really needed it, by setting up a Personal Pension Plan. Making sure that Joanna's material needs would be met were he to die first was important to Phillip, and the Personal Pension Plan took care of that, too.

■

You have now completed the seven steps of the GPS exercise, one by one, seeing the behavioral challenges you face when making important decisions and the behavioral solutions that help you overcome those challenges. You have witnessed the experience of two people, Francesca and Phillip, who have also done the exercise and came up with surprising (to them) insights into what they value in their life. And finally, you've seen the action items that Francesca and Phillip felt themselves compelled to do, which I then framed as general strategies applicable to everyone thinking about retirement planning.

I think you will agree that Francesca's and Phillip's experiences from the GPS exercise are a vivid demonstration of its efficacy in helping people discover what they care about and most value, things they were not fully aware of when they embarked on the exercise.

To conclude this book there are four short chapters. The first, "Other Applications of the GPS Process," is the story of my friend David, who used the GPS exercise to make a big life decision, namely where he was going to move to next, and who he would be with. This demonstrates the application of the GPS exercise to complex decisions other than planning for retirement. The second is a summary of the GPS exercise. Third is an afterword that looks briefly at applying behavioral science and behavioral economics beyond the challenge of setting goals. Finally, an appendix presents some potential action items for all the major retirement goals in the exercise. I said earlier in the book that this is not a financial plan for retirement. Working with an experienced financial adviser is the best way to accomplish that. Consider the appendix, instead, food for thought, a basis for continuing the conversation with your financial adviser.

■

Bon voyage on your retirement journey!

REFERENCES

Alzheimer's Association. 2013, Alzheimer's Disease Facts and Figures, 3.19.13.

Benartzi, Shlomo, Alessandro Previtaro, and Richard H. Thaler. 2011. "Annuitization Puzzles." *Journal of Economic Perspectives 25*, no. 4: 143-164.

Brown, Jeffrey R., Jeffrey R. Kling, Sendhil Mullainathan, and Marian V. Wrobel. 2008. "Why Don't People Insure Late-Life Consumption? A Framing Explanation of the Under-Annuitization Puzzle." American Economic Policy, Papers and Proceedings 9, no. 2: 304–308.

Brown, Jeffrey R., Courtney C. Coile, and Scott J. Weisbenner. 2010. "The Effect of Inheritance Receipt on Retirement." *The Review of Economics and Statistics* 92, no. 2: 425–434.

Kahneman, Daniel, Alan B. Krueger, David Schkade, Norbert Schwartz, and Arthur A. Stone. 2006. "Would You Be Happier If You Were Richer? A Focusing Illusion," *Science* 312, no. 5782: 1908–10.

Poterba, James M., Steven F. Venti, and David A. Wise. 2011. "The Drawdown of Personal Retirement Assets." NBER Working Paper, no: 16675.

Sass, Steven A. 2012. "Should You Buy an Annuity from Social Security?" Center for Retirement Research at Boston College, Working Paper, 12-10.

Shoven, John B., and Sita N. Slavov. 2013. "Efficient Retirement Design: Combining Private Assets and Social Security to Maximize Retirement Resources." Stanford Institute for Economic Policy Research, Policy Briefing, 3.14.13.

Van Boven, Leaf, and Thomas Gilovich. 2003. "To Do or To Have? That Is the Question." *Journal of Personality and Social Psychology* 85, no. 6: 1193–1202.

Webb, Anthony, and Natalia Zhivan. 2010. "What Is the Distribution of Lifetime Health Care Costs from Age 65?" Center for Retirement Research at Boston College, Working Paper, no: 10-4.

Whitney, Craig R., 1997. "Jeanne Calment, World's Elder, Dies at 122." *New York Times* 5 August.

Other Applications of the GPS Process

The Goal Planning System was designed with retirement planning as its primary objective. However, it can effectively help you employ a structured thinking process to tackle other complex decisions in life. And there are many, such as where you are going to live, which job to accept, or how many kids to have. And so on.

Here I'd like to introduce you to David, my friend from junior high. His story illustrates the application of the GPS system when tackling his biggest decision: Where is he going to live for the next few years of his life?

For pretty much as long as I've known David he'd planned to be a doctor, and he was sure he was going to live in Israel, get married, and have two kids. What happened to him?

Now in his forties, David is in the computer industry, lives in Manila, doesn't have kids, and has never been married. But for five years he's had a close relationship with a woman, whom he likes a lot. How many people do you think have made firm plans for the future at an early age, only to go on and do something completely different, just as David did? Many, I'm sure. Perhaps that includes you, too?

When I met up with David just recently, he told me that he had reached an important decision point in his life. He no longer wanted to live in Manila. Instead he was thinking about Tashkent, in Uzbekistan, as an interesting possibility, or maybe going back to Tel Aviv. But what about his girlfriend? He didn't want to leave her, but it was unlikely she would agree to leave Manila, because she had a very successful political career there.

David agreed to go through a somewhat-limited GPS process with me in order to help him decide what to do. This wasn't a formal process, more one friend helping another, albeit with a structured thinking tool at hand, with outcomes scribbled on a paper napkin over dinner.

In Step 1 of the GPS process, Identify Your Goals, David came up with three objectives for his future life:

> Family: get married, have one or two kids, build my own business, be healthier

I agreed with David that these were good objectives, but asked him if could come up with more. "No," he said. "That's my list."

I didn't have a formal Step 2 master list to show David, so I improvised. I know him well enough to have suggested a further option based on the fact that wherever he is, David is always socializing. He has a lot of friends and is always grabbing coffee, lunch, or dinner with someone. You get the picture. So I said to him, "How about loneliness, you know, not being able to have a coffee with friends, that kind of thing, something separate from family?" He responded immediately and said, "Of course. I don't want to be lonely. That should go on the list, too." I asked him if he would rank not being lonely as a secondary objective to the three he had initially thought of. He said, "No, that is very important to me. I don't know how I missed it."

David, a very smart and aware individual, had come up with what he imagined was a comprehensive list of goals that were important to him in his future only to discover that it was incomplete, just as Francesca and Phillip had. Avoiding loneliness had been a blind spot in David's thinking.

I then asked David to prioritize his four goals, or make trade-offs, which is Step 3 in the exercise. Given his limited set of goals, I only allowed one most-important and one moderately important goal, with two least-important goals. This is what he came up with:

- Most important: family
- Moderately important: health
- Least important: building a business and avoiding loneliness

With the above set of prioritized goals, what should David do? He's living in Manila and has a girlfriend of five years, whom he likes very much. Since family is most important to him, he could go ahead, marry her, and have children. He should settle down in Manila.

Easy. However, let's see what unfolded in the next few steps of the GPS exercise, beginning with Step 4, Think Beyond One Future.

I said to David, "OK, so far so good. Now let's go a bit deeper. Why don't you describe more than one future? Start with a really good one, one that is far above average. That's our Step 4A." David said he would have a wife, two children, be healthy, fit, and happy, and would have a lot of money.

I then asked David to imagine the other extreme, a really bad outcome, far worse than average (Step 4B). He said, "OK, I am lonely. It is scary, very scary." This scenario really caught David's attention and suddenly building a business and having money didn't figure so prominently in his thinking. Meanwhile, the prospect of loneliness loomed very large and he started leaning toward going back to Tel Aviv. Why? David grew up in Tel Aviv, served in the Israeli army, and feels at home in that city. More important, he doesn't feel lonely in his hometown.

This dramatic shift was the result of expanding his imagination beyond one future using a simple but powerful thinking tool, prospective hindsight.

Step 5 of the GPS exercise, you recall, is about predicting future preferences in life. You have already seen the answer to that, for David. When he was in high school David knew very clearly what he wanted in his future. He told me and his other close friends he was going to be a doctor, because that would give him the most career satisfaction. A few decades later, David had chosen computers over medicine and is having a blast in that world.

David is a very good example of the limits of forecasting, of knowing what we will want and what our values will be in the future. Were you any different?

The next step for David should have been Step 6, Consider the Perspectives of Others. As I explained earlier on, however, this was a rather informal version of the GPS exercise, done on a napkin over dinner, so I wasn't prepared with the experience of others. We therefore skipped straight to Step 7, Reprioritizing Goals.

As a reminder, this was David's prioritization at Step 3:

- ♦ Most important: family
- ♦ Moderately important: health
- ♦ Least important: building a business, and avoiding loneliness

Recall that when we went a little deeper, specifically in Step 4B, imagining a bad retirement outcome, David came to realize that Avoiding Loneliness was not just one of his goals but a *very* important goal. I wasn't too surprised, then, that when David had reprioritized his goals in Step 7, a big shift occurred. He said, "I now see that loneliness is the biggest issue for me, so Avoiding Loneliness has to be number one on the list. This is different from family. I need to have friends I can go have coffee with, lunch, generally be social. Family is separate from this."

Health remained important to David, because he wanted to sleep well and be active. At the same time, family and business were less important. So let's see David's reprioritized goals:

- ♦ Most important: avoiding loneliness
- ♦ Moderately important: health
- ♦ Least important: building a business and family

You can see, then, that family went from most important, which was to marry his girlfriend and stay in Manila, to being among the least important. Avoiding Loneliness, which wasn't even on his list to begin with, was now the most important goal. The only place he feels at home and not lonely is in Tel Aviv. So he decided to not marry his girlfriend in Manila and have children with her and broke up with her to move to Tel Aviv. (His girlfriend had been unwilling to leave Manila, as David had predicted.)

The GPS exercise moved David from one side of the globe, one culture, one relationship, to the other side of the globe, looking for another relationship, and feeling socially secure in his hometown, Tel Aviv.

I'd say that is quite a dramatic reprioritization in Step 7, wouldn't you? It is the result of expanding his imagination with this simple but powerful thinking tool of thinking beyond one future.

And overall, the structured thinking of the GPS process helped David see clearly beyond rather vague notions of what he *might* do next to what he really *wanted* to do next. That is the goal of the GPS process.

The GPS process worked well for Francesca and Phillip in helping them think about their retirement futures, and for David, in helping him decide where he was going to be for the next few years, and with whom.

How did the exercise work for you, given your own needs and values?

Summary

Most of us are familiar with the phrase, "To err is human."* And what we have learned in our journey through this book is that this ancient pearl of wisdom is indeed correct. To be human is to make errors of judgment and decision. More specifically, when we face the task of setting goals, we make two general errors. First, we typically don't think broadly enough. Second, we don't think deeply enough.

A good example of not thinking broadly enough was my rejection, more than twenty years ago, of an opportunity to be an early investor in a business that sold expensive coffee in a chain of homogenous stores. I simply could not imagine that this business model would eventually lead to a corporation with thousands of stores across the world and billions of dollars in annual revenues. My mistake was to focus narrowly on what was in front of me, which were my own preferences for what a good coffee shop would be like.

---

* From Alexander Pope's 1711 poem, "An Essay on Criticism." The complete line from the poem is "To err is human, to forgive divine."

I did not think broadly enough. I only envisioned one future (and obviously the wrong one).

Recall the tough decision that Robert, the hospital administrator, faced over whether to save Johnny's life or upgrade the hospital's diagnostic equipment. And recall that student observers were especially outraged when Robert took time to ponder the dilemma for a while, before coming to a decision. They simply did not want Robert to weigh the trade-offs he faced. The "right" decision was "obvious" to the students: Save Johnny. In this emotionally charged decision process, the students were making the mistake of avoiding trade-offs and therefore were not thinking deeply enough. Deeper thought would surely have weighed the potential benefits down the line of saving more lives, because of the presence of cutting-edge diagnostic equipment in the facility. To avoid confusion, I am not suggesting that Johnny be left to die, but rather that in the process of making the decision, difficult trade-offs will have to be considered.

To repeat, to be human is to make errors of judgment and decision. As we have seen earlier in the book, this is not because most people are lazy or stupid—absolutely not. We tend to make these errors because of the way the human mind works. It is a curious trait of human psychology. We fall into certain systematic thinking traps. This fact offers the opportunity for us to use insights from the fields of behavioral science and behavioral economics to help people avoid those traps: It gives us the Goal Planning System, which employs thinking architecture to guide us to make better decisions by helping us discover who we really are and what we really want.

We have seen many times that when people work through the GPS process, they find themselves discovering worlds that they had never fully imagined. They find themselves surprised by learning what it is they really want in their retirement years and being delighted with the result.

I hope that you have been surprised and delighted, too.

■

Below is a summary of the behavioral solutions—the seven steps in the Goal Planning System—that help address the thinking traps we face when setting goals as we make important and, perhaps, unfamiliar decisions.

THE SEVEN STEPS IN THE GOAL PLANNING SYSTEM:

STEP 1: Identify Your Goals: When faced with an important decision, avoid the trap of starting with Alternative Thinking and instead start by contemplating what you really care about. Employ the technique Ralph Keeney calls Value Thinking and start out by listing the goals that matter to you.

STEP 2: Discover Blind Spots: Refer to a master list of goals to come up with a more comprehensive list of goals and avoid inevitable blind spots in your thinking.

STEP 3: Prioritize Your Goals: Recognize that prioritizing goals can be emotionally and cognitively excruciating but having a guided process can make it palatable. When you do, be sure you are calm and not already emotionally and cognitively taxed by other demanding issues. You need all your cognitive resources available to make the best decisions.

STEP 4: Think Beyond One Future: In order to broaden your thinking, take a moment to imagine, first, what life would be like if your retirement went really well (Step 4A) and, second, what life would be like if your retirement went really badly (Step 4B).

STEP 5: Recognize the Limits of Forecasting: Acknowledge that your ability to predict what you will value in the future is limited by asking yourself whether, twenty or thirty years ago, you would have predicted your current tastes, preferences, and values.

STEP 6: Consider the Perspectives of Others: In order to overcome your limited ability to predict your future tastes and preferences, be open to learning from the experiences of others in imagining what your own retirement might be like. Again, the exercise can be applied to many domains, not just retirement.

STEP 7: Reprioritize Goals: Go through the Whiteboard Exercise, which is starting with a clean slate and reprioritizing your goals from scratch, without referring to your original list.

AFTERWORD: BEYOND SETTING GOALS

By now you already know that the Goal Planning System can be used when you face *any* important decision that involves setting goals. In particular, this seven-step system helps people think about their goals and what they really value and care about. In this book, I decided to illustrate how the system works by focusing on one specific domain—planning your retirement—because it is a challenge that most of us will face.

The development of the Goal Planning System is a first attempt to put some structure on our thinking, to help people make smarter choices when faced with important problems. Setting goals, however, is just one aspect of good decision making. I plan to use the tools provided by behavioral science and behavioral economics to help people think smarter in other ways, too. I am currently in the conceptualization stage of designing tools to help people think smarter about risks in our uncertain world. In the process, I will be looking for ways to leverage technology, particularly the use of digital technology and apps, to encourage smarter thinking. An early example of one such tool is a Loss Aversion Calculator. Loss aversion is a tendency for people to experience losses more strongly than gains. By going to http://www.digitai.org/#lab, you can try the Loss Aversion Calculator to measure how much more strongly you experience losses relative to gains. Thinking carefully about how you experience losses is an essential component of financial planning.

The Goal Planning System and the Loss Aversion Calculator are just two examples of what you might call "Thinking Apps." Given that we tend to think too fast, too narrow, and too shallow, it is time to use those little super-computers in our pockets to think smarter. After all, we now live on screens, so why not use them to improve our thinking. If done right, we can live a better life.

APPENDIX

If you have been using the Goal Planning System to think about retirement, at this point in the process you have generated a list of goals for your retirement years and you will have prioritized them, once in Step 3 and again in Step 7, following the rethinking Steps, 4–6. Now it's time for you to come up with a plan to help you achieve your newly prioritized set of retirement goals.

As I indicated in the introduction, I am not offering a financial plan in this book—that's a step best taken with a financial professional. Instead, what follows is a series of questions designed to help guide your next steps. The list doesn't pretend to be comprehensive. Rather, it is food for thought, an exercise to promote a productive conversation with your financial adviser for each of the goals you've identified.

GOAL #1 *If Financial Independence Is Important*

Should you put a "Personal Pension Plan" in place by considering financial products that provide guaranteed income for life?

Tip: Don't judge products like annuities* or drawdown funds by their labels; rather, focus on how they might help you meet your goals.

Should you defer claiming Social Security benefits? Claiming More Tomorrow makes the most sense for many people (Sass, 2012).

Tip: The lifetime value of Social Security benefits for couples, for example, can easily exceed one million dollars, so thinking about your claiming strategy is central to a smart financial plan.

GOAL #2   *If Healthcare Is Important*

Is your portfolio designed to keep track with the rising costs of healthcare?

Tip: From age sixty-five and on, the average retiree pays $260,000 out of pocket for medical expenses (Webb and Zhivan, 2010).

GOAL #3   *If Housing Is Important*

Should you consider downsizing to a smaller house, say "a two-thirds house"?

Tip: Don't forget to also consider the type of housing, such as retirement communities, which ensure you will not age alone and also addresses Goal #10 about social engagement.

---

* Full disclosure: Allianz Life Insurance of North America (Allianz), a sister company of Allianz Global Investors, is a leading provider of retirement solutions, including fixed and variable annuities and life insurance for individuals. Benartzi is Chief Behavioral Economist of the Allianz Global Investors Center for Behavioral Finance.

GOAL #4   *If Travel and Leisure Are Important*

How can you achieve the most enjoyable and memorable travel and leisure experiences from your new freedom?

Tip: You might enjoy much of the benefit of a change of scene from an excursion lasting five rather than ten days, but the costs may be substantially different between the two options.

GOAL #5   *If Lifestyle Is Important*

What sort of lifestyle can you realistically afford?

Tip: While many people die with virtually no assets, the wealthy often spend too little and live more abstemiously than they need to. Some should consider Spending More Today.

Should you try new experiences to better understand what drives your happiness?

Tip: My parents found out that changing diapers for the grandkids, and being involved in their upbringing, is extremely rewarding—and it's free.

GOAL #6   *If a Second Career Is Important*

Should you think about that other career you always wanted but never had a chance to pursue?

Tip: Don't focus on your former status at work or how much you used to be paid. Instead, broaden your thinking and focus on the type of work that would make you happier overall.

GOAL #7   *If Self-Improvement Is Important*

Should you explore who "You 2.0" is?

Tip: My father worked as a talented engineer for almost fifty years but he recently found out that he truly enjoys writing about philosophy.

GOAL #8   *If Family Bequests Are Important*

Should you think about "gifting now" instead of later?

Tip: Your kids probably need your help most while they are still young and trying to purchase their first home.

GOAL #9   *If Giving Back Is Important*

Have you thought about how much you might enjoy using your money and time to help others?

Tip: Prosocial behavior and spending make people happier (Dunn, Aknin, and Norton, 2014).

GOAL #10   *If Social Engagement Is Important*

Should you consider scaling down your work rather than retiring or consider a second career?

Tip: Apart from allowing you to maintain an income stream, continuing to work part-time could allow you to enjoy the personal contact that comes with it. Giving back in the form of volunteer activity could also provide this benefit. See also the comments made under Goal #3.

GOAL #11   *If Ending Life with Dignity Is Important*

When thinking about end of life, should you consider drafting a medical directive well in advance?

Tip: You might be surprised to learn that more than half of older adults in the US do not have a medical directive (Pollack, Morhaim, and Williams, 2010) and almost half don't have a will, either (LexisNexis, 2010).

GOAL #12   *If Control Is Important*

Have you planned a retirement environment where you can control your life?

Tip: Living somewhere that is within walking distance to shops, restaurants, and your kids instead of having to drive can make a big difference to your daily life. And for those living in a nursing home, research shows that simple activities—like being responsible for maintaining bird feeders—make people feel more in control of their lives and boosts happiness (Langer and Rodin, 1976; Banziger and Roush, 1983).

REFERENCES

Banziger, George, and Sharon Roush. 1983. "Nursing Homes for the Birds: A Control-Relevant Intervention with Bird Feeders." *The Gerontologist* 23, no. 5: 527–531.

Dunn, Elizabeth W., Lara B. Aknin, and Michael I. Norton. 2014. "Prosocial Spending and Happiness: Using Money to Benefit Others." *Current Directions in Psychological Science* 23, no. 1: 41–47.

Langer, Ellen, and Judith Rodin. 1976. "The Effects of Choice and Enhanced Personal Responsibility for the Aged: A field experiment in an institutional setting." *Journal of Personality and Social Psychology* 34: 191–198.

LexisNexis. 2010. "Lawyers.com Survey Reveal Drop in Estate Planning in 2009; Ailing Economy Likely Reason. http://www.lexisnexis.com/en-us/about-us/media/press-release.page?id=1268676534119836.

Pollack, Kalia M., Dan Morhaim, and Michael A. Williams. 2010. "The Public's Perspective on Advance Directives: Implications for state legislative and regulatory policy." *Health Policy* 96: 57–63.

Sass, Steven A. 2012. "Should You Buy an Annuity from Social Security?" Center for Retirement Research at Boston College, Working Paper, 12–10.

Webb, Anthony, and Natalia A. Zhivan. 2010. "What Is the Distribution of Lifetime Health Care Costs from Age 65?" Issue in Brief 10-4, Center for Retirement Research at Boston College.